# Look Beyond the Clouds

## Transform Your Daily Habits to Overcome Teacher Burnout and Find Joy in Teaching Again

### Michelle Gano

ISBN: 978-1-79-853673-5

# DOWNLOAD YOUR FREE JOURNAL!

---

## READ THIS FIRST

Just to say thank you for being the awesome human you are and for buying my book, I would like to give you the corresponding *Look Beyond the Clouds Journal* for **FREE!**

This journal offers a convenient space for you to write your responses to the Self-Reflect and Take Action sections at the end of each chapter. What a powerful record for you to revisit to measure your growth!

## TO DOWNLOAD GO TO:

www.lookbeyondtheclouds.com

*To Brandon—I am forever grateful for your unconditional love and support. Thank you for helping me chase my most precious dreams in life and for being beside me every step of the way.*

*It is a beautiful thing when a career and a passion come together. People with great passion can make the impossible happen.*

—Unknown

# Contents

# Introduction
## Join Me in the Sunshine

W arning: do not read this book like you are grading a paper. I know you can't help it, but just enjoy this! I know, I know. It's all part of the job, but let me explain! You spend enough time reading student papers, letters, emails, and notes to parents and administration. However, this book is different. *More fun.* I want it to feel like we're having a conversation. You spend enough time reading that kind of content, and I spend enough time writing it, so enough is enough. Let's have some fun being rebels together! Forget the amount of time you spend correcting papers. Instead, put the fancy red pen down and enjoy this.

~

Close your eyes. Think back to the moment you knew you wanted to become a teacher. All of the dreams and thoughts that rushed through your mind. Helping children learn everything they need to know to become successful in life. Helping them love learning and find the joy in working hard to overcome a challenging task. Helping them believe in themselves. Making a difference in their pure, innocent lives. Creating a safe learning environment where children feel supported, cared for, and important. Decorating a bright, cheery classroom that upon entering your children feel excitement to learn each day. Using fancy red pens to grade papers and give constructive feedback, so children can learn from their mistakes. Being a role model for them. Helping children tap into their strengths but also acknowledge their weaknesses. Teaching them how to be problem solvers, be kind to others, and strive to be the best versions of themselves. Being their champion—day in and day out.

**A teacher is ...**

A+ (I had to. It was too tempting.)
Amazing
Compassionate
Dedicated
Encouraging
Fun
Hard-working
Inspirational
Kind
Magical
Mindful
Organized
Positive
Reflective
Underappreciated
But most of all—exhausted

Able
Caring
Creative
Determined
Enthusiastic
Generous
Helpful
Intelligent
Loving
Magnificent
Motivating
Patient
Professional
Supportive
Misunderstood

Do those last three characteristics resonate with you? Do they remind you of a specific time when those feelings took center stage in your heart, classroom, school, or district? A flood of memories and emotions are most likely encompassing your mind. Isn't it astounding how that lengthy list of positives became quickly overshadowed by the negative?

Negativity has the uncanny ability to consume our full attention and silence the positive. It makes us overthink a situation and harp on it as we desperately attempt to wrap our head around why people behave the way they do or make the choices they make that impact others along the way. It takes over our precious mind, body, and soul ... *if* we let it.

That *if* is where the fire has been lit under my fanny. To help teachers feel genuinely happy again. To help us remember why we started teaching in the first place. To help us handle the day-to-day demands and do our best to avoid the dreaded teacher burnout. To make us feel important. Appreciated. Cared for. Supported. Understood.

## Never Alone—For Better or Worse!

You are not alone. Literally and figuratively.

*Literally*, you are never alone in your classroom. Ever! Even when your class is at their special and you ease into the unfamiliar silence, in walks a student who was sent back because they forgot something, got in trouble, who needs to pack up because they're getting picked up early with no warning at all, or they got hurt and are now in tears. And forget personal space! That's out the window the second your munchkins come barging through your beautifully decorated classroom door. My tip for this moment is a deep exhale and then follow up that overwhelming feeling with a smile.

One year, I had a student, let's call him James, who would find me *no matter where I was*. It was actually impressive. James had this ability of following my scent like an animal locating its prey; except in this case I was his prey ... well, not exactly. He was simply in need of much love and attention.

I would hear a knock on the door in those ten-ish quiet yet frantic moments before school began. I'd see his cute little face peering through the window searching the classroom up and down until he spotted me. The biggest smile would light up his face as he waved feverishly in hopes of a wave in return.

Without a doubt, *in* James would scamper ... every *single* time. Before I could even say hello, he'd be blurting a story from home or tattling about something that just went down in the gym where the students were lined up with ants in their pants waiting for the day to begin. In this moment, I would want to crawl into a deep hole, but, instead, I would politely nod, smile, and assure him that everything would be all right.

Some mornings I would try to hide (don't laugh ... you know you've done it too!), but sure enough James would find me. As much as this drove me completely bonkers, how adorable is it that he was *that* excited to greet me each morning (and get all of his stories out before the rest of the nuggets came in and he'd have to fight for time to talk)? It made me question if James was getting any attention at home. By the looks of it, he most certainly wasn't.

*Figuratively*, you are not alone in your daily struggles. Lunchtime arrives before you know it, so you can have conversations and make connections with adults for a change. Lunch in my school lasts for only twenty-five minutes. Then off we go to recess duty. It was twenty minutes the previous year, so look at us getting an upgrade! Those extra five minutes now consist of waiting in line for the one teacher bathroom while hearing the screams from the cafeteria on the other side of the faculty room door.

Even so, it's a nice break from finding yourself saying things like *I love you but let go, let go, I asked you to let go, I asked you to let go. Remember my personal bubble?* when they're so excited to see you that they hug a tad too tight. Or *Who's touching my toes?* when you're sitting in a circle on your colorful carpet trying to teach a lesson you've planned for all night. Or *Whoever pooped on the floor then smeared it on the walls better apologize to me by lunchtime since cleaning up is how I'll be spending my lunch ...* Yeah, I wish I could say I made up these examples.

## About the Countdown

Teachers are counting down the days each week, in between breaks, each year, and even to retirement. You hear it throughout the halls each day. One teacher recently commented, "Eight more years to go! If I've done fourteen so far, I can do eight." *Why do we live like this?* We shouldn't be simply pushing through each week and year, continuing on unhappy, especially when we have the most rewarding job in the world. I'm a tad biased, of course. We only get one life to live! This is not a dress rehearsal, people! Please, someone make sense of this!

More times than not, you give a colleague *the look* while passing them in the hallway with your ducklings following behind. The look usually consists of a loud sigh and wide eyes then a stiff smile that both points to and hides the frustration. A feeling comes over you that in that moment, they see you. They understand. You are not alone.

Teacher burnout and pure exhaustion are growing at a rapid speed in too many schools to count. So much that it is affecting our quality of life, schools, and education. **Now that the *problem* has been identified, we need to understand that *we are the solution.*** I feel a sense of responsibility to put my best effort forth in adding value and fulfilment back into teachers' lives.

We need to come together, start a positive movement, guide each other to a better outlook, and learn how self-care can prevent that exhaustion—and actually make the effort to practice it too—all while educating ourselves on how to remain positive in a stress-filled classroom. This epidemic needs to end, starting today.

Enough of feeling underappreciated, disrespected, misunderstood, and not taken seriously by administrators, parents, or even students. Enough of being unhappy and interviewing for different districts in hopes of a better situation. Many teachers end up leaving the profession because the extreme pressure hinders what they expected teaching to be. Teaching isn't simply teaching children anymore. Teaching is a profession in which you truly have to love what you do in order to continue to put up with the bullshit that's thrown at you from every direction each day.

That's one of the infinite reasons I refer to teachers as angels sent from above, superstars, and anything else that is magical in this crazy yet splendid world! Teachers should be treated like freaking royalty instead of being constantly questioned and demanded to prove ourselves with piles upon piles of data, paperwork, and over-analysis of our every move.

We're so focused on completing unnecessary paperwork for administration and figuring out how to get the students to behave and have an attention span longer than five seconds that we run out of time to *actually teach them*. Many days I wonder, *Are we data collectors or correction officers? Or are we teachers simply trying to make our mark on this world?*

In recent years, it has bothered me how this is accepted as the norm. As teachers we go about our days feeling overwhelmed by the high demands of our career while also feeling unappreciated and even mistrusted. I refuse to accept this, and I hope you do too. When I was hired, I was under the impression that I was fit for the job. We are under a microscope with administration coming in checking if we are teaching the lesson plan we submitted a week ago at the specific time we were given in our daily schedule. That doesn't make me a better teacher. It's a checkbox they have to fulfill. It's not to better our children's education.

After completing one of the most challenging and emotionally draining school year, I can't help but question—*what the shnikies is going on*? Exhaustion doesn't even begin to describe how I have felt each day. My munchkins required more love, attention, patience, and understanding than usual due to their horrific lives at home. Our classroom was their safe place, and I took that job more seriously than the academics aspect.

Since they felt safe and cared for, they were able to learn in my classroom (more on that later in this book). Every morning required concerted effort on my part to mentally prepare for the day. I sometimes wondered how I would find the strength to keep going back. Then I needed the following summer simply to rest and recover, so I was able to start up again in late August. I had to be ready for the new challenges ahead. My focus was to reset my power button over the summer and fight the urge to succumb to the power of teacher burnout.

Some may argue that because I'm in my late twenties and have taught for only six years, I don't know the full extent of teacher burnout. I agree. However, in my short teaching career I have experienced some of the darkest, most challenging situations. This past year in particular was the first time I understood teacher burnout and truly felt the lasting effects of it.

I always promised myself that being positive would help me prevent the oh-so-scary teacher burnout, but I learned just how hard it is to remain positive in a stress-filled, emotionally-charged classroom of the neediest, most precious children while also handling the demands from administration.

That leads to my point. If I am younger than my colleagues and newer to the field, why am I feeling the extreme effects of teacher burnout already? I would say to my husband every night, "I'm too young to feel like this! How am I going to do this for another twenty-five years?!" And there it was ... the *problem* we had to find a *solution* to.

My new life mission was then born: **if the education system and demands of teaching don't change, then we need to *be the change.*** We need to save our schools and teachers from becoming that haggard, crabby teacher (and I now understand why they are the way they are).

I could sit here and talk in detail about each trial and tribulation that left me in sheer amazement (unfortunately the bad kind), but that's not the mission of this book. The focus of my message here is quite the opposite. As easy as it is to get caught up in the complaining about and questioning of our high-pressure profession, I challenged myself to find the solution to our problem.

In this book, we will dig deep and discuss the positive chain reaction that can come from changed reactions to situations at work, the upward climb that is required in not only facing our challenges head-on but overcoming them to reach our breathtaking view, adjusting our mindset to think and speak more positively so that energy can inspire others to do the same.

We will learn how to *look beyond the clouds* that hinder our happiness, explore the power of gratitude for each experience, even the difficult ones, and learn to view them as opportunities for growth. We will push ourselves to step out of our comfort zone and be open to change, and to light our world by giving other people the gift of our presence.

We will master the idea of self-love by engaging in self-care practices ultimately leading us to dwell beyond the clouds in the brightest sunshine. Along the way you will regularly encounter self-reflection prompts as well as my recommendations for taking action. That's what you can expect from this reading experience.

Remember, it's all for our ultimate goal ...

**It only takes one person to start a positive movement, but it takes many more to keep spreading the message.** We are the solution to this problem. Be the change and remember we can't do it alone. I ask that you join me in helping both yourself and our colleagues rediscover the joy in teaching. Reconnect with our purpose. See the difference that our words and actions make.

I encourage you to enlist in an accountability buddy as you read this book. Let them borrow it, so you can read together and live out the positive impacts of this message. Spread the positivity to your classroom, school, district, and community. Quickly we will see the positive change sweeping the nation and world. I believe in this. In you. In us.

We will change the way teachers view their daily experiences. Help them—really, us—practice healthy strategies to better tackle each day with confidence and excitement. If we don't do this, then teachers around the world will continue feeling underappreciated and worn out. The demands of teaching and the education system are challenging enough. It's a job we need to love in order to do it each day while remaining sane. We need to come together and be the change. If we don't, it may never change. How tragic that would be.

In the eloquent words from the musical *Rent,* "No day but today."

# 1. The Chain Reaction of Changed Reactions

*Be the change you wish to see in the world.*

—Ghandi

What began as a date night ended up being one of our most unforgettable nights together. My husband's business made the signs for a new local restaurant in a small, rural town in New Jersey. We planned a dinner date there, which also happened to be the third night the restaurant was open.

Upon our arrival, we noticed there was only one waiter and two rooms full of customers waiting to be served. The owner frantically apologized to each table numerous times, explaining that the two other waiters hadn't shown up, so they only had one. We could tell he was trying to brush off the rude remarks from some of the customers.

It took about twenty minutes to be seated then another twenty to order drinks. Instead of complaining or making a scene like other customers did, we had the urge to help. My selfless husband, Brandon, and I looked at each other and voiced, "Be the change you want to see in the world, right?"

Without hesitation we got up and asked where they needed the most help. The restaurant owner looked at us in awe as if he couldn't believe his ears, quickly handed us notepads, and sent us on our way. Neither of us had any experience waiting tables. With smiles on our faces, we began! For the next four hours, Brandon and I waited tables, refilled drinks, cleaned up dishes, set tables, and most importantly helped everyone have an experience they would never forget. We quickly became friendly with the kitchen staff as we went flying in and out of the kitchen, putting in orders, serving meals, cleaning, and figuring out where everything was stored.

Brandon was a natural. He looked at the menu once and somehow knew the whole thing in detail. I, on the other hand, used my charm and humor as a way to provide a positive dining experience for the customers. When one little boy asked for a Jarritos soda, I replied, "Doritos?" Off to a good start. Oh well, I didn't promise to be the best at it. We were upfront with people, explaining we were customers just like them and saw the owner could use some help.

I'll always remember each person's reaction to that comment. They almost couldn't comprehend how or why we would do it. It was simply an instinct we had. We couldn't imagine how much time and hard work went into preparing this restaurant for opening night. We didn't want it to fail on night three! Looking back on it now, I hope it challenged the customers to look at opportunities in their own lives to step up and help others in need ... even for someone they don't know well.

Similar to what most acts of kindness do, ours created a chain reaction when another customer, Chris, was inspired to help as well. We got to know the customers on a deeper level. The power of human connection. They were interested in who we were and what we did for a living, which led to more meaningful conversation.

I remarked to one customer, Denise, "If only everyone spoke to each other the way we are right now, the world would be a better place."

Chris interjected by holding up his phone, declaring, "This is the problem these days."

I agreed. How can we communicate with the people right in front of us if we are too busy planted in our phones all day? I digress.

I worked closely with Clara, a young woman whose primary job was cleaning in the kitchen and clearing the tables. Clara and I became a power team. As we prepared place settings, she turned to me and apologized, "My English not good."

I replied, "My Spanish not good."

We laughed and had a full conversation in broken English and Spanish, and were able to learn so much about each other. She spoke about Guatemala and her family. I told her about my love for teaching and my amazing students in a low-income, Title 1 school. I told her that my students speak primarily Spanish at home and are currently teaching me basic phrases, so I couldn't wait to tell them I practiced this weekend.

If I say, "Yes, you can," when my students ask to go to the bathroom, they give me *the look*, and I quickly correct myself by saying, "Si, tu puedes." Then they're all smiles again. I love showing them that we are never too old to want to learn something new. Little do they know, *they* are the teacher too. I learn so much from them each day.

I was fascinated by the connection I made with this hard-working woman. Clara touched my heart in a way that I'll never be able to put into words. She brought me back to the international service trip I had the privilege of going on in Nicaragua where the language barrier presented a challenge but brought about beautiful human connections. Both of us were stepping out of our comfort zones.

We are proud to say, every customer left that night with a smile on their face ... even the ones who were originally irritable and flat-out rude to the owner. We continued to help clean up once everyone left. After four long hours, Brandon and I sat down and finally ate our own dinner. It was well worth the wait!

The owner and workers kept calling us their "angels." The feeling was mutual because that night made the greatest impact on our hearts. We couldn't stop smiling and reflecting on it from the moment we left ... to this day. As I passed Brandon a hundred times throughout that night, I kept thinking, *Wow, this is the person I get to share my life and build a family with! How did I get so lucky?*

My hope is that this story inspires you and many, many others to *be the change*. Be kind and compassionate human beings. Help others see the good in the world. Reach out to someone in need, even if they are a stranger. Think positively so positive actions can radiate from your soul—that energy will spread. Step out of your comfort zone. You may surprise yourself and uncover strengths and talents you never knew you had. Challenge yourself—you may learn something new. Believe in the power of human connection. Engage in meaningful conversation with other people by making face-to-face interactions a priority. You never know what you can learn from them.

The other customer-turned-helper, Chris, ended up being from my hometown in New York, which I had recently moved away from. We are all connected in incredible ways, but if you never put your phone down or take the time to meet new people, you miss out on the many opportunities that stand before us. I promise it will impact your life in ways you could never imagine. You will feel unstoppable, proud, and honored to help others. Take the first step on your journey of living a more fulfilling life and inspiring other people along the way.

## Right Here, Right Now

The fabulous Ellen DeGeneres says it best, "Be kind to one another." If everyone actually listened to those five simple words and put them into action, we would be living in a very different world. One that is more positive, accepting, compassionate, and understanding. One where violence and fear are less common. One where love is louder than pain, fear, and hatred. One where differences are embraced, not scrutinized.

As already shared, in this book you will learn simple yet meaningful ways to inspire yourself and others to navigate the challenging world of teaching with positivity and gratitude, address the issue of teacher burnout, and live in the sunshine. To remind yourself why you began teaching in the first place. You are responsible for your thoughts, words, and actions. **Start taking responsibility for your happiness. Not tomorrow. Not next year. Today.** I always teach my students that *you can't control what other people do, but what you can control is the way you react to it*. That's also one of my favorite responses to the good ole' constant tattling in class.

I've applied that same concept to navigating the world of teaching and the education system. In my opinion, the whole system needs to be revamped and completely changed, but that's a book for another time. Since it is very warped, it is easy to get caught up in trying to figure it out or change it or complain until something is fixed. The stance I try every single day to take is to focus on *the way I react to it*. It is easy to fall into the trap of wasting time and energy harping on the problems. I could go on and on too if I allowed myself, something that I have been guilty before of doing, instead of becoming the solution.

The message in this book wasn't simply written after a few years of teaching. It is a result of a lifetime dedicated to this profession. Rewind over twenty years back to a little girl who dreamed of becoming a teacher. I admired my mother's love of teaching and emulated her every move. At a young age, I would help her set up her classroom, grade weekly tests, and listen to copious stories of daily life in the classroom year after year. I learned a great deal from these stories about students, parents, administration, and education in general.

There was no question in my mind about it. I was going to be a teacher. Period. It's something that came naturally. I grew up performing in school plays, so I was prepared to apply those skills to my teaching as well. How else are you going to keep twenty-five kids focused and on task? I'm the crazy lady singing all the time and speaking in accents particularly during math lessons. If it keeps them listening and feeling excited about math, I will continue to do it all day every day.

Anywho, I'm tired of disappointing that little girl in my heart. It's time to bring awareness to this issue that is taking over the morale of our schools. I want us teachers to find the joy in our work again and be recognized for the super humans we are. We are responsible for our happiness. Let it begin with spreading the message of this positive movement. We can't do this alone.

If you are on board and excited to make a positive change in your own life, email me at michelle@lookbeyondtheclouds.com with the subject line, "I'm awesome and I know it," so I can welcome you to our fabulous mission and offer my help along the way. After all, you deserve to be both recognized and celebrated. Let it begin today.

Since you are so awesome, enjoy a free journal download from my website www.lookbeyondtheclouds.com to record your responses to the Self-Reflect and Take Action sections as you read the rest of this book.

## *Self-Reflect*

- When did you first become inspired to be a teacher? What led you to this decision?

- What words stood out to you most in the list of teacher characteristics?

- Which of your own teachers made a positive impact on your life? What positive qualities did they have?

- Which of your own teachers made a negative impact on your life? What negative qualities did they have?

- Now that you are a teacher, is it everything you thought it would be? What's the same? What's different?

- When have you felt underappreciated, misunderstood, exhausted, or unsupported as a teacher?

## Take Action

- List the positive qualities you want to exhibit at work each day.
- Create positive posters that will benefit your students—and yourself—in your classroom.
- Enlist an accountability buddy who will listen to your struggles but also challenge you to live the positive message in this book.
- Look for opportunities to be the change, the good in the world.
- Start taking responsibility for your own happiness. Remember, it is a choice.

# 2. The Upward Climb

*Don't tell God how big your mountain is. Tell your mountain how big your God is.*

—Anonymous

In today's world, children are faced with more challenges than ever before. They are exposed to adult issues at such a young age. If we push away the conversations because they cause you to stray from your oh-so-important lesson plan and claim that certain topics aren't allowed in school, then we're doing a disservice to our children. If they choose you to confide in, then consider you may be the only person they have to turn to. If you dismiss their concern, then they won't know how to properly cope with it in their developing minds.

Teach your students that they will be faced with challenges at home, at school, with friends, and in life. Help them know that they are capable of climbing any mountain as long as they have the right mindset. Teach children about setting goals. Model how it takes hard work, determination, perseverance, and self-belief to follow through with achieving a goal. Share stories from your own life about a time when you failed and had to pick yourself back up again. Many times children look at you as an angel who is pure perfection, but it's essential to show them how you cope in a healthy way with challenges you face.

## Your Magic Within

I recall a student in my school, but not in my classroom, who had more challenges than he was able to handle at such a young age. Let's call him Devin. He was afraid of germs to an extreme where it caused great anxiety and fear as he tried to navigate his way through each day. He refused to use any bathroom except the nurse's or the one in my classroom. His struggle was apparent as he cried each day in the middle of the hallway. My heart broke each time I saw this. It took a toll on his ability to learn as well as on his teachers' ability to get through a day successfully.

Our school secretary, who was simply an *angel*, would give Devin the love and reassurance he needed to be able to walk to his classroom each morning accompanied by a buddy. I witnessed this one hectic morning and saw how at ease Devin felt when she gave him "teacher magic." She invited me to be part of it, and from that day on, he would run to our hallway to get his teacher magic to start his day off right. Whatever helps, right? Cue survival mode.

This little cutie is a perfect example of a child who needs support beyond academics in school. The students in my class at the time would ask why Devin wouldn't touch doorknobs, why he would put his arms in his armpits after washing his hands, why he had another student walking him around the school, why he needed teacher magic, why he could only use our classroom bathroom, and so on.

I would provide simple answers about Devin not liking germs or how he enjoyed visiting our bathroom because our class was extra kind to him. Let's be real, Devin was treated like a famous superstar in my classroom. Each time he would come in, my class would all greet him and ask how his day was going so far. What was I teaching them with all of this? Acceptance. Understanding differences. Kindness. Empathy.

I grew to love Devin so quickly that I requested he be in my class the following school year. My principal seemed relieved knowing I was ready to give him the extra love and support he needed to continue growing and coping. I was graced with this opportunity and ready for the challenge.

One day a worthy explanation for teacher magic hit me like a ton of bricks: babies need magic from their parents and people who love them. Young children do too! This kind of magic helps after you fall while playing and get hurt, when you're scared at night and need an extra snuggle or lullaby. It even helps when you learn how to make your own choices.

As you grow up, you realize the magic has been in you all along. You just need to believe in it. This kind of magic helps you make goals, work hard, persevere when faced with a challenge, know the difference between good and bad choices. It helps you self-reflect, understand someone else's perspective, solve problems by brainstorming solutions, and use appropriate communication skills during arguments with friends or family.

If you believe in this magic when you are young, it will stay with you even when you are a teenager and an adult! Sometimes people will hurt you in life or not see your worth, but when you are strong, confident, and believe in who you are and what you stand for, that magic will be contagious and radiate from your soul. That light will spread like wildfire. Others will learn that they have magic inside themselves too.

That magic is a person's self-esteem, self-belief, and confidence. This magic makes you brave and have courage to persevere despite challenges. It gives you confidence to dream big and work hard to achieve each step along the way leading to your greater goals. It helps you face challenges with confidence and certainty that there's a way out. It helps you get back up again after you have fallen or failed in life.

This magic, self-esteem, is everything. If everyone was comfortable in their own skin, imagine how different the world would be. People would be more kind, loving, accepting, and understanding.

We can make baby steps toward that dream world by teaching our students and ourselves the power of believing in oneself. Remember that a positive movement starts with one person.

Teaching children coping skills and to visualize their breathtaking views, the dreams they have for themselves, is the essence of a successful path in life. They will face challenges and mountains, some more difficult than others. **If they can apply the strategies needed to handle situations in a healthy, productive way, then you are exceeding expectations as a teacher.**

Some challenges that come to mind are children learning to manage their behavioral diagnosis while feeling antsy, not in control of their body, being unable to concentrate. Disabilities or a language barrier will most certainly present a mountain for a child as well. Even something as common as getting new glasses or braces or a new haircut. This change can hinder their ability to feel comfortable and confident in themselves, making it more challenging to concentrate in school. Children will be faced with challenges while climbing their mountains, but the support of a teacher can make all the difference.

# One of My Mountains

How can you live a fulfilling life when you allow fear, challenges, insecurities, and wounds from your past to be in control of your present and future? Many people struggle with looking at the positive in a challenging situation and *looking beyond the clouds* knowing the sun will shine again. This is something I felt compelled to change. Not because I have lived an easy breezy life and have positivity radiating from my bones like people might think upon meeting me. Quite the opposite. I have experienced some of the darkest moments and situations that made me question if it was even worth it to fight. I lost myself in that darkness and didn't know how to find my way back. By the grace of a power much greater than me, I did.

I'll admit that simply the anticipation of writing about this past part of my life brings me anxiety. It's a place that my mind and my heart don't often revisit. A part of my past that ultimately changed my life for the worse (or so I thought). I've been hiding that part of me for over a decade, but in sharing my story I hope to help you and many others create light from such darkness.

This book is about positivity and finding the good, but the reality is many times we don't appreciate the light, the good, until we've experienced the dark moments and challenges.

During middle school, I remember struggling with exclusion from friend groups and daily ridicule as well as the lasting effects of September 11, 2001 on my family. I grew up in a loving family on Long Island. Children learn a great deal from their parents from a young age. I watched as my parents worked hard for the life we had. Family time was always a priority.

I also watched my family face tragedy on that fall morning. My father worked in World Trade Center 4, which was connected to the second Twin Tower that collapsed. I can't begin to imagine what he saw that day. His goal was to see his family again like everyone else. Helping others along the way, my father made the last subway and train to Long Island.

However, he lost very close friends during the attacks. That's a difficult realization to have. That day changed my family and my life forever. Yes, our father came home to us, but life in my family became different—it felt more tense. More broken.

I had always been the silly, playful girl who loved to make people smile. It would break my heart when other people were upset. My immediate reaction would be to help them and make them laugh. This innate ability of mine grew more difficult each day. I started to lose who I was at my core. Needless to say, I did not handle this tragedy very well.

**The sadness that surrounded me every day started to creep into my mind and take over.** I would yell when there was tension or anger, and I would cry out for attention and reassurance that everything would be okay. In the midst of more yelling, my heart couldn't take it anymore, and I would scream, "I just want to kill myself!" I figured the pain would finally go away.

That bold statement would stop us all in our tracks. This became a theme, and I found myself struggling to find happiness the way I used to so easily. I wasn't thriving. I was simply surviving. Day in and day out. Stripped of the happiness I once knew. That is no way to live.

I didn't put much thought into how or when I would actually harm myself. However, I felt very uncomfortable around kitchen knives because in the back of my mind I knew that could be a way out. I became fearful of them because my mind would go places I knew my body would never be able to handle.

I struggled in the new family dynamic that consisted of walking on eggshells around each other as each of us grieved differently. Although my parents did what they thought was best at the time, I didn't respond well.

They sent me to a therapist for quite some time to work through this period of my life, but it didn't help because it wasn't on my own terms. I think my whole family would have benefited from seeing a therapist to help us each cope in a healthy way. Thankfully, we have come a long way since then.

## The Healing Power of Music

Music saved my life. It helped my mind escape. To feel and express the intense emotions. The power of music became my saving grace, my coping method. I remember listening to my iPod with tears streaming down my face as I curled up in a fetal position against the wall every single day. This is when my faith took center stage in my heart. Whether you are a believer or not, that is okay. I like to think we can all agree that there is something greater than us, a higher power of some kind.

I struggled with relationships and friendships. As soon as I sensed drama or unnecessary tension, I would feel triggered and remove myself. I spent most of my teenage years feeling lonely and wishing to be my happy self again. No matter where I was in life and how dark things seemed, there had to be a breathtaking view out there for me. *God is just waiting to surprise me, right?* This thought kept me fighting.

It wasn't until I was a bit older that I realized that the key to a happy life is looking for the light when you are faced with tragedy. Each obstacle we face in life can be viewed as a tunnel. If we continue to work through it, we will reach the light at the end. I was broken, yet hopeful.

Responding to tragedy and coping is a challenge everyone faces throughout their lives. Some people find healing in positivity and faith. Others were never taught how to cope in a healthy way. Notice the word *taught*. This skill needs to be taught and modeled for children, and many times they see unhealthy ways of resolving conflict at home or on TV. As teachers, we can be that positive role model in their lives. They need us to be a light for them in this damaged world.

If you haven't heard of the radio station K-Love yet, I highly recommend you go look it up. Right now. It's positive, encouraging, uplifting, and all things magical. I happened to come across this station one day in my car, and the friendly voices were rallying listeners to begin a thirty-day challenge. Catching my attention, I turned up the volume.

The challenge was to listen to only K-Love for thirty days anytime you were driving. Initially, I wasn't sure if I wanted to take a break from my other music and singing away, making everyone around me think I was nuts. That thought quickly passed as I found myself agreeing to this challenge and actually feeling excited to begin. I knew I was in need of positivity and encouragement in my life at the time, so I was all in. Ready to rock and roll. Well, not quite, but you get my gist. Ready to be inspired and tap into an unfamiliar calmness in my heart.

For thirty days, I fell deeply in love with this challenge. So deep that I went beyond the thirty days. Now, I'm going on ten years! The music and encouraging words fill you with positivity, peace, inspiration, motivation to be your best self, reminders of hope, and a power much greater than yourself. Since music has always been my rock, what better way to grow deeper in my faith and heal than through music? Every once in a while, I'll switch around to other stations, but I always find myself coming back to K-Love. Even if you don't consider yourself a religious person, the inspirational and positive tone will certainly add value to your life.

I remember listening to the radio on my way to work the morning after a school shooting in our country, and K-Love shared an inspiring viewpoint: *we're used to praying for answers or blaming the higher power we believe in, but instead we should pray for the strength to be the answer.* There's that powerful phrase again to *be* the change you wish to see in the world. It is after an incident of deep tragedy that you see people begin to work together and be there for one another.

Brainstorm how you can make a difference in your own school. Plan lessons centered around kindness and community. Reach out to the students who seem lonely, and encourage students to do the same. Make positive steps toward a safe and loving learning environment. Create a team of teachers and students to spread the message of love and acceptance. Discuss the importance of coping strategies and giving one another support. I welcome you to share your successful strategies as well as concerns with fellow teachers as well. You can post your ideas and questions on the *Look Beyond the Clouds Community* on Facebook—or you can email me personally—michelle@lookbeyondtheclouds.com. Rest assured, I will respect your privacy in our communications.

You know your students best and how to address certain situations in an age-appropriate manner. It's never too early to teach children how to face challenges and overcome them with healthy goal-setting and coping skills. Many children lack this knowledge, which is detrimental to our future society. If they're unable to problem solve or cope in a healthy way, they are going to lash out, fight, and potentially cause damage to themselves or others.

I created an area in my classroom for the children to go when they need a break. The purpose is to help them monitor their own emotions and acknowledge when they need a break. Positive and motivational posters and children's books fill the space along with a flip chart of healthy breathing techniques and ways to cope with overwhelming emotions. One chart lists the simple ways they can calm themselves, which include write about it, draw a picture, breathe deeply, rest your head on a desk or pillow, remember a happy time, take a brain break, read a book, do mindful coloring, complete a puzzle, and count to ten.

There is a bin of sensory items they can use to help calm themselves, such as small stuffed animals, stress balls with various textures on them, and a mirror to analyze their facial expression and recognize which emotion they are feeling. Setting a sand timer is one way to help the child become responsible for rejoining the class after an appropriate amount of time. Check out www.lookbeyondtheclouds.com to see photos of this break area.

When children experience trauma on any scale, it takes a toll on their ability to learn and remain focused. If this space gives them the break they need to recharge, then I am all for it! It is my hope that they take these simple coping strategies into the big world as they grow up and find themselves facing all kinds of challenges.

## Self-Reflect

- What fears, challenges, insecurities, and wounds from your past do you allow to be in control of your present and future?
- What coping strategy has helped you after a tragedy?
- Think back to a time when you felt lonely as a student. Who helped you? What did this teacher or classmate say or do to help?
- Think of a time when you, as a teacher, felt lonely or in need of encouragement. Who helped you? How can you continue the chain reaction and help someone else?

# Take Action

- Acknowledge and find peace with the fears and wounds from your past that cause limiting beliefs.
- Find out what radio station K-Love plays on in your area and start the thirty-day challenge.
- Brainstorm ideas with your class on how to promote kindness and establish a loving, supportive classroom community.
- Reach out to the students who seem lonely, and encourage students to do the same.
- Create a team of teachers and students to spread the message of kindness and acceptance.
- Discuss the importance of coping strategies with your class.
- Create a corner in your classroom where students can go for a break when needed. Make motivational and coping strategy posters together.

# 3. *Your Breathtaking View*

---

I magine standing at the base of a volcano being told you were about to begin a journey to the peak then slide your way back down on a thin wooden board. Volcano boarding began with our guide's encouraging words, "Show yourself what you're capable of doing." Those words ignited a spark in me as I stood at the base of Cerro Negro Volcano during my service trip in Nicaragua.

Up until this moment I didn't fully realize the magnitude of this climb. All I knew was that volcano boarding was like sleigh riding, except on an active volcano. No big deal, right? The reality quickly set in that this was going to not only be physically challenging but mentally challenging. It required a mental strength I wasn't sure I had. With a long wooden board and water bottle in my hand, it began. Ready or not, up I trekked.

Instead of looking up at the top of the volcano taking in its massive size, I chose to look down at each small step I took. I kept repeating phrases to myself like *baby steps, you can do this, one step at a time.* I was good at tricking myself into believing I was mentally strong enough for it. Fake it until you make it, right? I was by no means in the best physical shape for this task, but I focused on having the right mindset. Sometimes that's all it takes to overcome challenges, doubts, or fears.

Memories of my past experiences with the Tough Mudder Challenge raced through my mind. Instantly, I felt strong and more positive. If I could run twelve miles and tackle twenty-five military-style obstacles with almost no training *twice*, then I could get myself through this too. Crossing that finish line was the best feeling of accomplishment. I was ready to prove to myself that I could reach that rewarding feeling again. This gave me the boost of confidence I needed. A gentle reminder of the magic within me.

What else was running through my mind other than planning my unrealistic exit route if the volcano decided to blow? Music, my favorite therapy. I was singing away in my mind. Songs from *Rent*, which is always a go-to for me. Songs about fire and struggle, and I softened it up with "The Climb" by Miley Cyrus and Disney songs. Whatever kept my feet moving, I sang for me, myself, and I, and enjoyed every minute of it.

My inner child was intrigued by the "sleigh riding" part with many questions left unanswered. I imagined how fast I would go. *Hmm, maybe that's how I can escape the hot lava if necessary!* With each passing thought, onward and upward I moved. Higher and higher until the car we'd ridden in looked like an ant on the ground at the base of the volcano.

One last challenge lay ahead before reaching the ever-desired top. There was a thin walking trail connecting us to the top. All we had to do was not slip and fight the strongest winds to cross it! How bad could it be? Now would be a good time to mention I am the world's biggest klutz. So clumsy that I trip on myself while walking on a flat surface.

Even worse, I once ran straight into a wall at my neighbor's house when I was in second grade because I was so excited to go outside to play Spice Girls and draw a road out of chalk to ride our bicycles on. That marked stitches part three all within a few months … all on my face. I digress.

With that in mind, picture how confident I felt inching across that thin trail. Not so much. My plan consisted of A) not panicking, B) looking straight ahead and not down, and C) praying like crazy. But really, I had angels looking out for me on this one.

*The winds whipped and my stomach churned.*

*Baby steps. You can do this. One step at a time. Keep your head up. Ahhhhh, I peeked! Don't look down, I repeat, do not look down.*

*(Exhale) You got this. This is a breeeeeze. Ahh, don't think about that part! Is someone going to grab me if I slip? Oh dear God, please send me a sign! What the heck am I doing up here? Too adventurous. Nope. No more. Why can't humans fly, so I can fly off of this thing?*

*(Exhale) I'm home on my cozy couch wrapped in a soft blanket. Safe and not about to FALL INTO AN ACTIVE VOLCANO.*

*(Exhale) Pretend you're a graceful not-clumsy-at-all ballerina balancing impeccably on the balance beam in a pretty blue, sparkly tutu.*

*(Exhale) Muuuch better. Glitter and all things sparkly. Hey, we made it across! That was easy!*

Little did I know, the breathtaking view awaiting our arrival. Words can't even begin to describe what I saw as we stood at the high peak. Pure amazement. Wonder. Awe. Beauty. Faith. Hope. The view from the top of the volcano that almost just kicked my ass made all of the moments of catching my breath, panting, and fighting off the wind worth it. All it took was baby steps and determination and positive thoughts. Or mostly positive with the exception of the *slight* panic dancing around in my head as I lived out my sole ballerina experience.

A profound realization came over me in that moment: we are always going to be faced with mountains in life (or in this case, a volcano). Some might last for a day while others might last for months or years. Don't allow yourself to view the entire mountain at once. Acknowledge that it's there, then determine your first step for starting the climb to reach the top, proving to yourself that you *are* strong enough.

Your ability to overcome these obstacles is what builds your character and determines your life. *Baby steps, you can do this, one step at a time until you reach your breathtaking view.* Just as Cerro Negro wasn't even the largest volcano in the group, sometimes we view our challenges as the worst possible, yet others have it far worse than what we are experiencing, so we should remember to be grateful for what we *do* have.

If you'd like to see photos of this adventure, you'll find them at my website: www.lookbeyondtheclouds.com.

~

Sometimes I wish I could jump back into that moment and relive it all over again. I often reflect on what my breathtaking view is in life. The most sublime moments. The moments I achieve my most precious dreams and accomplish my goals. I want you to take a moment to do the same. Pause in your reading to imagine your dreams coming true. Close your eyes and visualize it.

Now determine the first step you need to take in overcoming your mountain and reaching that goal, making your dream a reality. **Have the courage to take the first step. You never know**

**what view you will miss if you don't.** Anticipate your breathtaking view. Work hard to reach it. I promise you won't regret it. You are much stronger than you think you are. Give yourself more credit. There are highs and lows in life, people who choose to do good in the world and people who choose to do bad. Choose wisely and take that first step.

As I stood at the base of the volcano, all I could see was black ash and rocks. Then the view from the top of Cerro Negro was absolutely breathtaking. A vivid image that will stay in my mind forever. Similarly, no matter what obstacles you've had or darkness you've lived through, the view is sensational once you reach it. Don't forget to appreciate each simple moment and baby step along the way. Those small moments lead you to the breathtaking view.

Once you're at the "top" of your life, personally or in your career, the view is going to be breathtaking, even more so because of the struggle and experiences you overcame to get there. This brought such peace and meaning to my life as I looked out at the most beautiful view.

Imagine your breathtaking view at work. It can be observing two students problem solve after a disagreement during recess without asking for your assistance. It might be your students successfully doing their part in making your classroom a kind and productive place to learn. It can be helping that one student who has been struggling in math to understand a challenging concept after weeks of practice and repetition.

Your breathtaking view may be doing well on an observation lesson or getting your dream teaching job after a long interview process. It can simply be accomplishing the list of demands from administration each week, such as lesson plans, documentation logs, communication logs, behavior logs, data collection, updating your class webpage, correcting weekly tests, and so on, by Friday afternoon, so you can take a break from work on the weekend.

Breathtaking views—both simple and grand—will start to catch your attention if you open your eyes to them. Life doesn't have to be so hectic and planned. Sitting, talking, laughing, and taking the beauty in each day at home and work is more than enough. No matter what your breathtaking view includes, remember to take a deep breath and determine your first step. Keep going. Keep pushing yourself. Fall and get back up. Take the next step. **Your breathtaking view awaits.**

As I imagine my breathtaking view, these simple moments come to mind. The moments I wake up next to my husband each morning. I cherish it and squeal inside as if it's the first time. The moment I saw my baby for the very first time. It's incredible how you love these little humans even before you get the chance to meet them and kiss their pudgy cheeks!

The moment I experienced my first day of school as a teacher. The moment I swam with dolphins. The moments I spent in Jamaica and Nicaragua serving other people and learning so much about life, love, and joy. The moment my husband and I moved into our first home after building it as a team for six months from the ground up. The moment I hold this book in my hand after it is published.

Other cherished breathtaking views include the nighttime skies I encountered during my service trips to Jamaica and Nicaragua. I had never seen so many stars all at once. Standing there in awe among such beauty. Millions of stars shining brightly as if they were spotlights from Heaven. I couldn't believe that's what we miss at home.

The simplicity of these moments captivated my attention. I knew I'd always remember the warm air, light breeze, the sound of trees blowing in the wind, and the dirt covering my body from the day's activities. I had never been that covered in dirt before in my life, but I also never felt that beautiful before either. Beauty is in your character and how you spend your time. There was something so special about being with people and truly not caring about appearance. Pure happiness and laughter filled our precious moments there. Now, that's quite a breathtaking view.

~

Visualization is a strategy you can use for yourself and with your students. It is visualizing what you want to achieve. Picturing yourself accomplishing a desired outcome or goal, and living in that moment as if it were really happening. Who is with you when you achieve your goal? What is happening? Where are you? When is it occurring? How are you feeling?

When you practice visualization, you are more likely to accomplish your goals because feeling it, living it, breathing it in, helps motivate you to take the necessary steps toward your goals.

You can use visualization for goals that are big or small. You may visualize the moment you hit "submit" on your report cards or the moment you finish your last parent-teacher conference without a hitch. It can be watching the light bulbs go off in your students' brains after nailing an awesome lesson or activity that took a few extra tries for them to finally understand.

I challenge you to dig even deeper. Visualize feeling genuinely happy while driving to work and excited to start a new day of teaching. Handling the day-to-day demands while avoiding the overpowering feelings of exhaustion or being worn out. Visualize your principal, students, or class parents verbalizing their appreciation for all that you do.

Visualize yourself taking the time for some much-needed self-care to renew your energy and spirit. Navigating the challenging world of teaching with positivity and gratitude. *Looking beyond the clouds* that hinder your breathtaking view and choosing to live in the sunshine. Visualize yourself taking responsibility for your happiness and adjusting to a more positive mindset.

Regardless of what you or your students are visualizing, that simple act will help motivate and lead you to the results you want to achieve. Try it today!

Setting goals and taking action is something that needs to be taught and practiced. It is a muscle that needs to be strengthened. The best way to remain motivated in navigating the world of teaching with positivity is to gain the support and encouragement of a trusted teacher friend, an accountability buddy. This is someone who believes in you, supports you, cares about you. It's also someone who will give you the tough love you need to stay on track. Remember it's a two-way street. You will believe in them, support them, and care about them the way they do for you.

Once you accept responsibility for your actions, you are one step closer to reaching success. **Goal setting is the easy part. Following through is the challenge.** You can set up weekly meetings or phone calls with your accountability buddy. Honesty is the best policy when it comes to your check-ins. It's called an "accountability" buddy for a reason. They will hold you accountable. That's what you want them to do! It's amazing what you can accomplish when you don't want to let someone else—and yourself—down.

Make a commitment to not use the words, "I'll try" when attempting to meet a goal. Instead, use the words, "I will." You either achieve the goal or you don't. The choice is yours.

# My Clouded View

As a young girl, my dream was to be a teacher. This never wavered. I knew I would do whatever it took to make it my reality.

After several years of teaching, I started to lose sight of that dream. My breathtaking view was clouded by frustration and exhaustion. This terrified me. I knew teaching was what I was always meant to do, but my focus seemed to shift. I began to feel like a zookeeper managing behaviors all day and hearing parents balk, "Not my child!" Or being told by administration that consequences cannot be used as discipline anymore. I'm all for positivity, but children—and everyone, really—need consequences!

How could my view of teaching become altered so badly, especially when I'd always known I wanted to be a teacher? What was clouding my clear view? Those constant challenges and struggles that drive so many of us teachers to feel hopeless ... and to even drink wine straight out of the bottle! I'm referring to myself on this one, but I know there are others out there. I'm not alone!

My personal favorite is RELAX Riesling because it tells you in large print on the bottle what to do: relax. *Okay, you don't have to tell me twice!* I can picture the way the bottle glistens under the counter lights. The striking blue glow. I can hear the crisp sound of the cap twisting off. Yes, I know I'm classy with my twist-off bottle of wine. Who has time for corks after a long day of teaching anyhow?

The realization that my take on teaching had become dark and moody lit a fire in me so strong I couldn't ignore. I suddenly discovered a passion and desire to make teaching better. To make teaching enjoyable again not only for myself but for you. Now I am on a mission to get all-star teachers like you on board to make a positive impact for teachers around the world.

Together, we can reach as many students and teachers as possible. Why? Because this message matters. *You* matter. If we improve the world of teaching, then education for our children will improve. Sure, I realize our big and bold goal is slightly terrifying, but it's worth every ounce of energy and moment of our time. If we don't do it, who will?

Take a moment to consider if you are taking steps toward your biggest dreams in life and in teaching. What is it that makes you feel alive, both as a person and as a teacher? What part of teaching and our education community makes you want to jump out of bed when you wake up? What aspects of teaching motivate you to be your best teaching self? Are you living to work or are you working to live your life and accomplish dreams?

It's easy to lose sight of your greatest goals and ambitions for teaching and for your whole life because things change, dreams change, then life happens. We get comfortable or accept that "things got in the way" of our dreams. Many people seem to settle rather than strive to be their greatest most fulfilled selves. They find themselves saying phrases like *I wish I could* or *Maybe one day.*

No. Just no. I won't allow you to count down to the weekend each week and go through the motions in your classroom. **Don't waste your life thinking there's a good enough reason why you have given up on your teaching dreams.**

# *Self-Reflect*

- What mountains or challenges have you faced in life? In your career?
- How did you push yourself to keep going?
- What breathtaking view do you visualize as you reflect on your teaching goals?
- Has your view been clouded by negative experiences? If so, how can you overcome this with positivity and practice?
- What makes you want to jump out of bed in the morning and start your day off on a positive note? Is it a favorite song or a special person you want to see?
- Who motivates you in the classroom and at home to be the best version of yourself?

# Take Action

- List your top five teaching goals. Put them into three categories: Accomplished, Work in progress, Life got in the way.

- List the baby steps you need to take in order to accomplish each goal.

- Post your goals in a place where you will see them every day, even if that means putting them on your phone's home screen.

- Share your goals with your accountability buddy for additional support and motivation.

# 4. Being a Blue Balloon

Imagine a large garbage bag of twenty blue balloons. Each balloon is filled with helium. Because they are weightless, all of the balloons are moving in the same direction—*upward*. This is what happens when people are positive and work together toward a common goal. They seek to find solutions to problems. Being supportive and encouraging helps everyone to move upward to reach success.

Now imagine a red balloon filled with water. If that red balloon is placed in the same large garbage bag with the twenty blue balloons, what will happen? You guessed it! The bag will begin to descend rapidly. The weight of that single red balloon will impact all of the other balloons and bring them *down*. Being competitive, negative, or not being supportive will hinder your ability to meet your goals and will hurt everyone in your proximity.

Picture this concept in your own school and district. Who in your school is a blue balloon? This includes administrators, teachers, other staff members, students, and parents who are positive, supportive, and helpful. Those who greet you in the morning or reach out when you are upset. Those who lift you up.

I was fortunate to have a positive, hard-working principal. She did every job under the sun in our school—from acting as the lunch aide for an entire year when we couldn't secure one of our own, to covering classes when we didn't have enough substitute teachers, to sweeping and mopping floors, and much more. She went above and beyond to keep the morale afloat even when tension rose within our district. Team building was always a priority to her and the positive effects of that were evident.

I learned too that sometimes the decisions administrators enact are out of their control and unfortunately they are just the messengers from the upper administration in the district. It was heartbreaking to watch this incredible blue balloon principal reach a bursting point due to the red balloons above her.

Even after her tireless effort, her balloon had been deflated and she left mid-year for a new district. Notice that making this change was worth it in order to remove herself from negativity. In a way, I was happy to see her go because I know she deserves more. She should be in a district that appreciates her and respects her enough to recognize the heart and soul she puts into her work every single day.

Who in your school is a red balloon? The people who are negative, complaining, and unsupportive. I'm sure they come right to mind. They are quite easy to spot. Those woe-is-me folks who spend their time making their life situations sound worse than yours as if it is some competition. Let them have that victory because it probably *is* far worse with *that* outlook! Do their negative words and actions bring down the morale of your school? Even the children can easily spot this among their teachers or classmates.

One year a student confided to me, "I wish all of the good kids could be in a class together, so we could actually learn without distractions. It's not fair to us." She was right. It wasn't fair. Similarly, I've found myself yearning for a professional development day regarding self-care practices in which all the "blue balloon" teachers who sincerely want to better themselves and enhance their teaching skills could be grouped together while the "red balloon" teachers be placed in a separate room, preferably on the other side of the school.

Which balloon are you? Take time to reflect on this. Be honest with yourself. Also identify the people in each category at your school. Once you've come up with a list, I encourage you to make a conscious effort of spending more time with the blue balloons. You exhibit similar qualities as the people you spend the most time with.

Therefore, if you spend time with people who are positive, kind, and good listeners, you will start to see those qualities in yourself. If you spend time with red balloons and hear them being Debbie Downers about anything and everything, you will start to think in that way too. Choose wisely. Your life depends on it.

## Silence Please!

Silence the negativity. Don't you sometimes wish life was like a cell phone where you could put it on airplane mode, kick back, and relax? Even though we necessarily can't do that, especially in the midst of a chaotic day at work, we can do our best to take in the negativity that surrounds us, then choose to silence it. In order to feel positive in a stress-filled school, you must rid yourself of other people's negativity ... and your own. Acknowledge it and help others when you can, but then refocus yourself on the good.

I remember shoving my lunch down my throat while also trying to catch up with my colleagues, all the while just moments away from my long-awaited bathroom break one Monday afternoon. A fellow teacher uttered, "Ugh, is it the weekend yet? Isn't it sad that this is our life and we're just wishing it away every week because we don't want to be here?"

I understand that not every teacher falls into this countdown tendency, but it saddens me to think that many do. I'll admit that I let myself fall into this countdown in my own head at times. I also admit that hearing these little comments throughout the years of my teaching career has served as a big motivation for me to write this book and help spark a change for teachers.

A common reality in many households is a lot of noise and sometimes (or in some cases, most of the time) yelling. A strategy I've taught my students is to listen to music. Music = therapy. As I already mentioned, music has always helped me and always will. There is something special about hearing a certain song that can change and improve your whole mood and outlook on a situation.

I give you the same advice—whether it's your colleague or simply your own mind—drown out that noise and negativity by listening to positive, uplifting music. Blast it and sing as loud as you want for all I care! That's what I do. And guess what? ... It works. Not so well when your baby is taking a nap or your students are taking a test, but daze off for a moment, reconnect with a positive thought in your mind, or picture yourself dancing to your favorite song, then—voila!—notice the smile that lands gracefully back on your face.

There are two types of people in this world. People who choose to be positive and people who choose to be negative. Positive blue balloon teachers may be that way because—while they experience difficulty at times—they still choose to find the good in order to remain happy and content in their career. Negative red balloon teachers may be that way out of fear of failure, not being good enough, or fear in some other capacity.

Sometimes teachers who tend to be negative have a hard time seeing teachers who are positive and living happily. They may want everyone to feel the misery they feel. Be positive anyways. Maybe after some time, you will inspire them, and they will follow your lead by making small, positive changes in their own life.

## The Powwwah!

Three things, or as we like to call it "free fings." Back when my husband, Brandon, and I were dating in college, he would listen to my endless to-do lists as I tackled twenty-one-credit semesters on top of being very involved on campus. The first year we started dating also happened to be the year I was taking sixty credits in order to graduate on time (more on that later). He is certainly a keeper!

As he could see me getting overwhelmed, trying to manage it all, he would ask, "What are three good things that happened to you today?" This simple question would stop me in my tracks and make me remember the good moments, what really mattered. I would go along with his brilliance and quickly feel at ease focusing on the *positive*.

After college, we were dating long distance for three years. During that time, this simple question became the focus of our nightly phone calls. We looked forward to this. Throughout the day, I would take note of the good I found and write it down, so I wouldn't forget in the midst of the stressful moments. Once we moved in together, that was—and still is—our go-to dinner conversation each night. It's amazing to see how the perception of your day, the words you *choose* to use, can change your whole mindset.

Focusing on the three good, positive, magical moments from your day helps silence the nonsense or challenges you face. Many times we stress about little things that we make into a bigger deal than they need to be. Yes, it's important to acknowledge the challenges and talk them out, but I've learned (the hard way) that harping on them won't necessarily make them any better or go away any faster.

Instead, figuring out if there is a solution to the problem or a way to make it even slightly better is all it takes. You can even modify this idea by starting with something stressful then following up with your three things from the day. Always end with the good.

Ultimately, it's up to you. **You have the choice to use positive words that highlight the beauty in each day or negative words that emphasize the bad, stressful moments.** When you choose to give power to the negativity, it can take over your mind and cause you to fixate on it. This can cause you to lose sleep at night because your mind is racing as if you're in the lead of the Daytona 500 NASCAR race.

It can also negatively impact our relationships with others. Who wants to spend time with someone who is always a Debbie Downer? Not me! That, my friend, is no way to live. Instead, think of the phrase (in a singing voice of course), *I've got the powwwah!* Say it loud, say it proud because you *do* have the power.

Which one will you choose today? Tomorrow? Next week? Next month? Okay, you get my gist.

~

Smile. It really is that simple. "Smile before bed, you'll sleep better." I read this saying while on my first international service trip. I was immersed in the marvelous culture of the Jamaican people but living in conditions much different from home. I was amazed at how there were no glass windows, just bars to keep everything out. Except bugs ... very large bugs. Uncomfortable? Yes. But life-changing? Absolutely.

Experiencing a new way of life gave me a whole new perspective on needs versus wants, and the true quality and meaning of life. I remember covering my body and face with a sheet to fall asleep in hopes of no mosquitoes finding a way to bite me. I certainly had to practice this saying of smiling before bed. I would focus on my three things from the day, and all seemed well with the world. I knew I was surrounded by opportunities to learn and grow, so I chose to embrace them with my whole heart.

It amazes me when teachers finish the words *I need* with something that is more of a *want*. Challenge yourself each day to live simply by distinguishing between what you want and what you actually need. I'm not saying you shouldn't ask for school supplies or materials when you need them. What I am saying is to *be grateful* for those things.

I am amazed by some topics of complaint made at work when I've seen schools that don't even have pencils or crayons or a matching set of educational workbooks for their students to use. One example of this is when someone acts like the world is ending when their SMART Board doesn't work or the internet goes down, making it impossible for students to use their Chromebooks for a lesson. Or when the faculty room is now too small and crammed because a couch was put there by our thoughtful blue balloon principal to offer seating beyond just the hard table and chairs. I sometimes wonder if these kinds of teachers think before they complain and consider if it is a need or a want.

While on this service trip in Jamaica, we spent most of our time at a local school and a nursing home. One day our group leader, let's call him Tom, went up to a man who was doing yard work and offered a hand. Tom helped him rake leaves into bags. They stood together and spoke for a while. I noticed the man was missing his nose and eight of his fingers.

I was curious to hear his story. Little did I know what he was about to explain. We had the pleasure of meeting this special man, Lloyd, later on that day. His openness and ability to be vulnerable was inspiring. He shared his life story with pure honesty.

Lloyd was in an accident where a tractor's engine exploded and flung him off. He was in the hospital for a year and a half recovering. He came to live at St. Monica's Nursing Home when it first opened in 1982. He remembered his first day so vividly. September 17th. He was diagnosed with Hansen's disease, also known as leprosy. It was heartbreaking to hear Lloyd repeat, "Why? Why me?" I'm not an expert on leprosy and how it comes to be, but I share with you the words Lloyd spoke that day.

After he finished his story, Lloyd asked, "Do you think you could go through what I did?" I couldn't help but replay that question in my mind and reflect on its depth. From years of self-reflection, I've learned this powerful concept: we all have our own story and struggles, but we each find our inner strength to overcome those obstacles.

We move forward remembering where we came from and how we found the strength, courage, and determination to face our struggles head-on. **It's not about what we are given (or not given) in life, it's about how we *choose* to look at it and handle it.** Positive thinking leads to positive action. Cultivating this ability to persevere regardless of our challenges and pain is the key to a happy and healthy existence.

Lloyd did exactly that. He struggled with his diagnosis at first, then decided to put his energy toward something positive and productive. With his bare hands he built a greenhouse in the backyard of the nursing home and has maintained it ever since despite his crippling disease. It was truly remarkable to see the detail in its construction and design. He used any small tools he had lying around to create this masterpiece. Please go to www.lookbeyondtheclouds.com to see photos of Lloyd's remarkable greenhouse.

Lloyd beamed with pride as he described his greenhouse and gave us a tour of the numerous rows of vegetables he was growing. Everyone could use this reminder in life. People who have far less than you live in the riches of choice, positive thought, and life's beauty and simplicity each day. Focus on the good moments when faced with a challenge.

One of the Jamaican group leaders on this trip gave us an inspiring talk before a local school band performed to thank us for our visit. He spoke of how he views the colors on the Jamaican flag, which are black, green, and yellow. There may be struggles in life, but the grass is still green and the sun is still shining. (Now that lovely kid in the class who questions everything you say or do would demand, "Well, what if it's cloudy?" To that, I'd reply, "Ah, yes, but remember, my sweet cherub, that the sun is still shining even *beyond the clouds*.") Anywho, positive thinking leads to positive actions, so start your journey today.

Catch yourself when you recall a good moment during your school day. Celebrate, congratulate yourself, do something that will make you feel like the fabulous teacher you are. Cue your happy dance! What a glorious way of looking at each day we are given in life. We can either feel bad for ourselves when we feel worn out and choose to be unhappy, or we can find the good in each day, in each moment we are gifted with our students.

## Teacher Tats

A snapshot moment is something good that happens where you take a picture of it in your mind, in hopes of cherishing it forever.

It's something that makes you stop wherever you are and squeal, *This is amazing!* Or *I love my life!* Your heart feels so full and your smile can't get any brighter as you possibly (most definitely) break out into your go-to happy dance.

Other times a snapshot moment leaves you in awe of something breathtaking, such as a colorful sunset, a star-filled night sky, watching your baby sleep so peacefully in your arms, or even a funny moment in your classroom that you can't help but give in and laugh with your class. These are the moments that leave an everlasting impression, or shall I say "tattoo," on your heart.

How often have *you* felt this way in your classroom, school, and beyond? Some of you might be thinking, *Umm never ... where can I get me some of that life?* Others might be thinking, *A few big days come to mind like my wedding, the day my baby was born, when I went skydiving, when I first laid eyes on my adorable puppy, when I bought my first home, when I took a trip of a lifetime—but nothing from teaching.* Only a handful of you are thinking, *Oh that's easy ... only every single day!*

Imagine what our world would be like if more people had that last reaction. Picture the amount of love, excitement, and purpose that would fill the air! All of that would lead to more positive vibes and kindness. Schools and classrooms would be filled with teachers and students who look for and appreciate those snapshot moments, which would then encourage even more!

Regardless of how you responded, starting today you now understand the choice you have. You can continue living an okay, mediocre life because you're comfortable enough with it or you don't want to take chances. Or you can step out of your comfort zone, look for those breathtaking moments, and truly change your outlook on life for the better, in your classroom, school, and beyond.

By being more positive, you've *got the powwwah* to change the lives of the people around you each day. When you smile and wish your students and colleagues a good morning, you give them a glimpse of the good they desire, the positive energy, even for only a moment. It will make them feel so warm inside that they'll want to do the same for someone else. Then—boom! A chain reaction has begun.

~

Be patient. Change won't come right away. Changing your mindset is like developing a new habit. It takes time and consistent effort. Continue to focus on the good each day to help get you there sooner. Acknowledge other people's concerns—students, colleagues, family, and friends—sympathize with them, understand their perspective, then challenge yourself to find the good in the situation. I wouldn't recommend you suppress the negative. Instead, acknowledge it and refocus on the positive. This will help you stay on the path to attaining positive energy in your classroom and at home.

By no means am I saying it'll be only rainbows and butterflies every day. There will be difficult situations and challenging days that shake you to your core. **Simply remember, there is good in every day. We just need to open our eyes to it and recognize those snapshot moments.** Appreciate it with the utmost gratitude. In these moments of recognition, you are well on your way to attaining a more positive outlook, so you can move upwards like the blue balloon teacher you strive to be. Spending time with other blue balloons will help encourage you to develop more positive habits, which will then lead you to notice the good, positive experiences in your classroom and school.

## Self-Reflect

- Which balloon are you? Blue or red?
- Are you bringing positivity or negativity to conversations at school? What about at home?
- Do you choose to spend your time with blue balloon teachers or red balloon teachers?
- What makes you smile before you drift off to sleep? Have a go-to thought when you find yourself unable to smile before bed. Mine is humming as I picture the ballroom scene from *Beauty and the Beast*.
- What are your three good things from school today?
- Was there a snapshot moment at school today for you?

## Take Action

- Create a list of people who are blue and red balloons in your school. Make an effort to spend more time with the positive blues.

- Talk about your three good things from your school day during dinner with family or friends. If you are by yourself, write about them in a daily journal.

- Celebrate the snapshot moments you experience —whether they are big or small. Remember, they will create a strong foundation for your positive and joy-filled teaching career.

- Be patient. Changing your mindset, both about being a teacher and about your life in general, takes time and consistent effort.

- Acknowledge other people's concerns, sympathize with them, understand their perspective, then challenge yourself to refocus on the good in the situation.

# 5. Airplane Abyss

On a cloudy, dreary day in Miami, Florida, we set off to our final destination of Managua, Nicaragua. As the plane ascended into the sky, it pierced through the thick clouds. This amazes me more and more each flight I take. As we rose beyond the clouds, we were greeted by the brightest sunshine. I found myself fully embracing this moment. Closing my eyes as I took a deep breath in (hoping no one was sneezing around me), then gazing out at the abyss while slowly exhaling. Breathing in and out. In and out. Taking in the breathtaking view. The warmth. The beauty of our world. The wonder.

I noticed the sun beaming into the small airplane windows and gracefully landing on the faces of strangers around me. I noticed soft smiles on their faces as if they were taking in the sunshine just like I was. I noticed the fluffy clouds floating by. Some larger than others. Scattered across the ceaseless sky. I imagined myself jumping on each one as if they were trampolines.

That wonder suddenly left me in awe. A realization came over me as I soaked in every moment. **Even when some days seem cloudy or difficult, the sun is still shining *beyond the clouds.*** Even if you don't see it now, it's still there. On those dark, challenging days when you don't feel that warmth, it's there and waiting patiently to greet you again. You simply need to believe that it will come again and choose to *look beyond the clouds*. In that moment, my new favorite motto was born ... *Look beyond the clouds*. Hope remains. Even on the darkest days, the sun will show itself again.

## Mindful Morning Meetings

Picture the morning in your students' homes, and even in your own household as you get your children out of bed, fed, dressed, and on their merry way to school or daycare. Typically it is a hectic time. As soon as the children get to school they are sent into another whirlwind of unpacking their belongings, handing in their homework to be corrected, ordering their lunches for the day, starting their morning work, and having the urge to socialize and catch up with their friends all while being told to hurry up so attendance and lunch count can be taken, homework and important notes from home can be collected, and finally lessons can begin.

We, as teachers, set routines and structure, or "organized chaos" as we like to call it, but many times we overlook the need to take a moment to breathe and ground ourselves before the day begins. Our body breathes automatically, so we tend to forget to simply be in the moment and take a few deep, healthy breaths.

That is exactly what I use morning meetings for. A time where students can feel acknowledged, important enough to be heard, and loved, so real learning can take place that day. You will appreciate this time with your students removed from academics as it also stimulates their brains, so they are ready to learn.

I have been fortunate to work in a school district that encourages the use of a morning meeting each day. In a perfect world, it consists of a quick greeting among students, a morning message from the teacher, and an opportunity for students to share a story or opinion about a given topic and participate in a group activity.

In reality, I use it as a way to come together as a class family and acknowledge the start of a new day in a calming way. It can last anywhere from ten minutes to thirty, depending on the to-dos of the day.

Another way of implementing quick, yet meaningful "mindful mornings," as I like to call them, is having a set topic for each day that allows you and your students to think deeply about things that often go unspoken. I will share my version of "mindful mornings." You can make adjustments to best suit your class.

**Memory Monday:**

Share one story or fun news from your weekend. (Emphasize *one* or you'll be sitting there for forever trying to cut them off as you listen to the play-by-play of their weekend.)

**Thoughtful Tuesday:**

Say something kind about yourself or a classmate.

**Wishful Wednesday:**

If you could make one wish come true this week, what would it be and why? (It can be academic or personal.)

**Thankful Thursday:**

Share something or someone you are thankful for today and why.

**Fun Friday:**

Reflect on your week. Share a moment that stood out to you. A moment that made you want to break into your favorite happy dance.

If you prefer an "afternoon closure," you can have students reflect on and share something good that happened that day as they line up for dismissal. Being mindful and taking time to breathe and reflect with your students can make all the difference in their personal and academic success.

~

John Lennon was speaking my language with his "Imagine" song lyrics, "You may say I'm a dreamer, but I'm not the only one." Some negative people used to tell me I was a dreamer and lived in a fairytale world in my head. I felt so misunderstood. They had this undertone that it was a bad thing, but look where that positive mindset and *looking beyond the clouds* has led me. I now look at the phrase "being a dreamer" as a compliment because that's exactly what my life turned out to be: my dreams coming true.

I've tried my best to remain focused on having a positive outlook and *looking beyond the clouds*, and as a result, I find myself on an enthralling path in life. When other people see sickness, see it as a way to learn about health. When other people see a dead end, see the narrow path beside you leading a different direction. When other people see rain, remind yourself that it's just water and see the puddles you can jump in.

When teachers are faced with change, I see it as a challenge accepted and an opportunity to grow. When a teacher is allotted the most difficult student, see it as an opportunity to get to the root of the child's behavior issue and help them learn how to cope.

Thinking positively and *looking beyond the clouds* doesn't mean you are a dreamer. Instead of telling children (or adults) to stop the dream world in their minds and snap back to reality, encourage it. Choose to focus on the light at the end of the tunnel even in dark times. Visualize the life you want to live versus the life you are living now. Visualize the classroom or school you want to work in and help create it one step at a time. Don't lose sight of the vision you pictured teaching would be.

## Cultivating a Growth Mindset

A "growth mindset" is the belief that your abilities can change through effort and hard work. It's the perspective that mistakes are opportunities for learning. A "fixed mindset" is the belief that your abilities are the way they are and cannot change. People with a fixed mindset are fearful of making mistakes. Review the lists below to see the difference between a growth and a fixed mindset. It illustrates how to turn negative statements into positive ones. **If you change your words, you can ultimately change your mindset.**

| **Instead of Thinking** | **Try Thinking** |
| --- | --- |
| This is too hard. | This may take some time. |
| I give up. | I'll use a different strategy. |
| I made a mistake. | Mistakes help me learn. |
| It's good enough. | Is this really my best work? |
| I will never be able to do this. | I will learn how to do it. |

There are several books that explore the growth mindset, and I plan to write one of my own, but my favorite one to date is the children's book *Bubble Gum Brain* by Julia Cook. The story's two characters are Bubble Gum Brain and Brick Brain. Brick Brain uses negative words and doesn't believe in himself. He is too scared to try anything new. Bubble Gum Brain uses positive words and challenges himself to never give up. He teaches Brick Brain how to think in a positive way and achieve more positive results in life.

My students love this book and visualizing Bubble Gum Brain versus Brick Brain. I teach them how to apply it in their daily lives. I hear them referring to each other as a Bubble Gum Brain when someone works hard to accomplish a goal or problem solves when they get stuck on a math equation. I also hear them encouraging each other to not be a Brick Brain and keep trying.

I use a Growth Mindset Word Wall to introduce three new vocabulary words per month, and we incorporate them into our morning meetings, lessons, and daily conversations. By the end of the year, my students are exposed to new words that positively impact their lives. Some sample words from this activity include *determined*, *effort*, *obstacle*, *challenge*, *learning*, and *mindset*.

If you're into cooking like my handsome husband is (hallelujah!), then treat this like a recipe. Listed above are all of your necessary ingredients to make this delicious life you desire. (Read the following using an announcer's voice) *Get your apron ready because you are about to create ... the most positive, encouraging classroom in your school!* If you want to think even bigger and greater than that, then you are about to create ... *the most positive career—and life—and inspire other teachers to do the same!*

If that doesn't tickle your fancy, think of it as the playbook to your real-life Super Bowl. Or the dress rehearsal to your sold-out Broadway show. Now I'm speaking my own language ... theatre, singing, dancing, performing, and all things magical. Whichever way you choose to look at it, all of these simple concepts can be applied to your life and teaching. It will add value to your students' lives as well as your own. **Positive *thinking* leads to positive *words*, which leads to positive *actions*, which leads to a positive *life*!**

I use these concepts in my own classroom and notice such a difference between the bond I establish with my students compared to other classes. I also notice the difference it has made in my personal life and how I view teaching. These practices really do work. They teach my students and me to always strive to be the best version of ourselves. That, in turn, positively impacts the world even after my munchkins grow up and leave my classroom each year.

Take the time to recognize those simple snapshot moments in your classroom. Appreciate them. Praise them. Celebrate them. You get more of what you focus on. Most days in a classroom feel like chaos, rushing from one lesson to another and checking the clock to make sure you're doing what you're supposed to be doing based on a confusing and unrealistic schedule made for you by administration.

My favorite days are the ones in which I notice something good happening and I say, "Screw the schedule! This is more important." Take the time to live in that moment. Soak it in with your students. When I do this, I find myself saying things like, "Wow, I love my job," a lot more often, and my heart fills up again as I am able to breathe and simply *be* in that moment. If something funny happens in your classroom, remember to let loose and laugh with your class.

The simplest moment can shift your mood drastically. Write these moments down after they happen so at the end of the day you can read that list—short or long—and be reminded of the good. Recognize and appreciate these snapshot moments with the utmost gratitude. **It is the moments you used to dream of while studying to become a teacher.** Be fully present. Be a Bubble Gum Brain.

Teach the adorable youth of today how to reflect, be self-aware, and focus on the good. If you don't, society will continue to be filled with negative whiners who think they're entitled to everything. Do you really want that? Me neither. Children are never too young to start encouraging positive thoughts. Once these practices become habits, then we've hit the jackpot. So let's get this positivity train out of the station, and see who else we can bring along for the ride.

## Self-Reflect

- Think of a challenging situation you are facing in your life today—at school or at home. It can be big or small. What positive thoughts and phrases can you use to *look beyond the clouds*?
- What are mornings like in your home and classroom?
- Are you a Bubble Gum Brain or a Brick Brain?
- What can you do today to think and speak like a Bubble Gum Brain would?

# Take Action

- Start your day tomorrow with a morning meeting in your classroom. Use my guide to help you get started!
- Make a list of negative thoughts turned positive. Catch yourself when you use a negative version and repeat it using the positive version. Encourage your students to do the same.
- Plan a short lesson for your students about growth versus fixed mindsets. Teach them about the list of negative thoughts turned positive. Post that list in your classroom and refer to it daily as a reminder to use positive self-talk. Make this an ongoing topic and theme in your classroom. Monitor your progress together to see if you are reaching that growth mindset as individuals and as a class.

# 6. Growing Through What You're Going Through

---

*Appreciate the people, situations and things that you don't like because without them you wouldn't have clarity as to what you really want.*

—Anonymous

Have you ever questioned why certain events happen to you, especially when they pose such challenge or heartbreak in your life? This is true for your personal life and your experiences in the classroom. I believe each child on our beginning-of-the-year rosters was put there for a reason. It is our job to uncover why. Each child, and person, in our life is there to help us learn and lead us to who we are meant to be. When I think about it, I see this is "growth mindset" thinking!

Every teaching experience you have had from being a substitute to a teacher's assistant to a full-time teacher has shaped you into the educator you are today. This chapter is a friendly reminder, that gentle nudge, to be grateful for the lessons you've learned along the way. We encourage our students to learn and grow each day. Don't forget to do the same for yourself. You deserve it.

My first year of teaching was something I had visualized and dreamed of since I was five years old. I grew up playing school any chance I could get. My mom was a teacher, so she decked out our basement and created a dream classroom, including desks, a bulletin board, a chalkboard, and many themed decorations. I would play school for hours.

As I got older, I even used this as a way to study for my own tests in (real) school. I would pretend to teach the information, and that was my way of learning and memorizing. I knew if I could teach it, then I understood it enough to do well on a test. Except with geography. There's no hope for me there. I knew teaching was in my future, and I couldn't wait to grow up and take in the breathtaking view of my *very first classroom*.

I began college as a middle school math major with the plan of teaching this unique age group. After my sophomore year, my career vision changed slightly after I failed a calculus 2 or 3 course. I don't even remember which course it was, likely in hopes of blocking it out of my memory for obvious reasons! However, this F led me to where I am today, so you guessed it … I'm grateful for it. I had the highest GPA, and now I had an F? You could imagine that didn't sit well with me. I knew it was a sign that this wasn't the right path for me.

I decided to change my major to elementary education. In Pennsylvania, this means I can teach birth through fourth grade. As you know, this varies depending on which state you get certified in. Can we take a minute to laugh about that? I picture a mother pushing out her newborn and me being there, announcing, "I'm certified to teach your baby!" Anywho, I went forward with this plan with hope in my heart and a clearer vision for my life.

When I presented this change in teaching direction to my college advisor, it was as if I was asking to go from one major that was polar opposite than the other. I expressed my desire to complete this change but still graduate on time, and she quickly shut this idea down, telling me it wasn't possible.

*Challenge accepted!* She didn't know what I was capable of when I set my mind to a goal. I knew at some point I would be grateful for her making this difficult because it lit a fuego under my fanny to prove her wrong and prove to myself that I *could* do it.

I quickly rose to the challenge, telling her I *would* be able to accomplish it and I would show her how. I don't believe she liked that very much, but sometimes you need to stand up for yourself and believe in yourself even when others don't.

I reviewed all of the remaining credits I needed to take over the next four semesters and created a schedule which would work based on the available course days and times. I presented it to her each semester pretty much doing her job of figuring out the "how" for her, and she simply had to sign off on it. Thanks to my dad, I had a lengthy, color-coded spreadsheet to make this process easier. God, I love color-coded anything, especially spreadsheets!

That first year consisted of a twenty-one-credit semester followed by nine credits during a winter session, another twenty-one credits in the spring, then finally nine credits during the summer. Along with this packed schedule, I also had to complete over one hundred observation hours in various local elementary schools.

Simultaneously, I took and passed the three tests needed for certification in New York. As a junior, I had already prepared myself for the move back home and started the certification process there. As mentioned earlier, this was also the year I met and started dating my husband. I quickly knew he was a keeper!

I am proud to say I completed sixty credits in one year in order to graduate on time and didn't let anyone tell me I wasn't capable of accomplishing this. I knew I was. **I promise that when you set your mind to do something, you can do it!** Don't let anyone's negativity get in your way. My greatest achievement senior year was when I was the sole recipient of the Excellence in Education award at graduation.

Guess who couldn't look me in the eye or congratulate me? Yes ... that lovely, encouraging "advisor" of mine. I proved her wrong and excelled beyond measures to achieve my goal with the support of all of my incredible education teachers. They were like mothers to me. Truly special women who set such an amazing example of how to teach with your whole heart.

I thought the challenges were behind me.

I graduated on time as planned. I spent the first few months after college as a permanent substitute teacher then quickly earned a teacher assistant position in a math academic support room. Watching the light bulbs go off in each child's head was simply the best. Having the freedom to be creative with new activities that would make learning fun with a hands-on approach made my life as a teacher wonderful.

I spent my nights at school earning my master's degree in literacy education. Knowing it was a three-year program, I marked that as the goal for ending the long distance portion of my relationship with Brandon, my then boyfriend. Summer came and I had two years left before making the much-anticipated move to New Jersey to begin my and my husband's life there.

An opportunity came up to interview at a Catholic school for a full-time teaching position. I figured I would gain two years of full-time experience, which was difficult to find in a public school in New York, and then I'd bring that experience to a New Jersey public school.

The awaited phone call came a day after the interview. I answered the phone to hear the principal ask if I would accept a kindergarten position for that coming September. All I could do was cry the happiest tears of joy. This was it! *My dream come true of having my very first class.* I immediately pictured a classroom full of precious little munchkins whom I would always remember as my first class. Kindergarten wasn't my ideal age group, but I was willing to jump in and make the best of it.

The excitement of my first full-time year quickly turned to negativity. The clouds started rolling in. I wanted to continue implementing new teaching ideas and strategies, but I was told not to stray from tradition. What one teacher did we all must do. So much for creativity and differentiation, right? That didn't sit well with me because I knew it wasn't best for the children.

The realization settled into my heart that I would never earn the respect or support from my colleague, let's call her Kate. Her class seemed to be full of the "good" kids since she had a student in her class with well-known parents in the community.

Meanwhile, my class felt like a circus on most days. I dealt with the most challenging, defiant, and constantly disruptive behaviors to the point where I would go home with a migraine daily and cry to my poor angelic husband on the phone each night, yearning for support from Kate, who was my so-called "mentor."

I was in survival mode. Not quite how I imagined my first year of teaching to be.

Instead of wasting my energy on her negativity, **I chose to focus my energy on finding the things I could be grateful for.** I created the most warm, loving, and supportive environment within my classroom. I had a wonderful teacher's aid and fellow colleagues who supported me through it all. The most special bond came from this change as I found the good in each child. A school family was formed.

What I found during that year was how the students act as teachers too. They taught me about patience, empathy, and unconditional love. Those challenging students ended up being my greatest accomplishments. The bond we formed was our key to success. They learned from me because they felt safe and loved. I was able to teach them because the feeling was reciprocated.

I built them up with insurmountable love and encouragement, helping them respond in incredible ways. I loved these children as my own. Fighting for services and support for these cuties from the principal was my focus because I knew what they needed in order to be successful.

This was supposed to be the happiest year for me when I was finally becoming the teacher I'd always dreamed of. Instead, it was a year of exhaustion and trying to prove my worth, knowing it would never be appreciated. Pure disappointment settled firmly into my heart at times. I felt broken and unappreciated for going the extra mile day in and day out to do what was right for "my kids."

I remember driving in my car during the last week of school, desperately needing those next two months to recharge and find peace from the chaotic school year. I cried and prayed to God, saying I couldn't go through another year like that if Kate were still there. She would take every opportunity to go out of her way to make herself look good and for me to look like a failure. What she didn't realize was if I failed, so did she as my mentor. I guess that is a lesson for another day.

The next day at work, I found out through the grapevine that Kate was leaving the school. I took the biggest sigh of relief and cried tears of joy this time. God had answered my prayer. I had such peace knowing I could have a fresh start and enjoy my second full year of teaching. All I had to do was focus on the good and remember how much I had grown already.

Through each trial and tribulation, I learned to overcome the obstacles in my way. I didn't just become the teacher I had always dreamed of. I became *even better* because of the challenges I faced. I grew tremendously that first year because of the hardships. The big takeaway for you: stay true to yourself and always do the right thing. Stand up for yourself and your students when the time comes that you need to. When you do the right thing, you'll be able to go to sleep each night with a clear conscious. **Find the good in each student, laugh with them, and love them endlessly.**

That second year was the complete opposite experience since I had the most incredible fellow kindergarten teacher to work with. We planned each week together, decorated our hallway beautifully, and always found ourselves singing and making up dance moves to songs for our classes. Her bellowing laughter was contagious and filled our hallway with such joy. She was a true gift and still is to this day. Even though we are miles apart now, the memories we created together for our students will last a lifetime.

If you are ever asked to be a mentor for a new teacher, please put yourself back in their shoes of starting out somewhere new and be as helpful and supportive as you can be. Be the kind of colleague you want others to be to you. Kind, supportive, encouraging, helpful, understanding, knowledgeable, and all those fabulous qualities we teachers possess.

If you are a new teacher, communicate your needs with your mentor, so they know how to best support you. Be open to new ideas, but also embrace your creativity while lesson planning. Be a good listener and appreciative. If you don't mesh well with your mentor, take in what you can from them and know who else you can go to for support in your school. There are plenty of amazing teachers out there ready to help you see the good and help you thrive rather than just survive. No matter what your age or experience level is, always be willing to be a mentor for other teachers and seek help when you need it yourself.

I'm grateful for the challenges I faced in my first full-time year of teaching because now I go out of my way to help new teachers in my building and even other districts to make sure they never feel the way I felt. We all have our own style of teaching and personality, but we all share the common goal of doing what is best for our little munchkins. Remember that.

~

It's amazing how God weaves the experiences of our life in a way we don't always expect but that lead us to where we are meant to be. On October 10, 2013, I got one of my favorite surprises to date. I had always been inspired to go on a service trip because of a man named John. He was a family friend of ours who had moved to Nicaragua many years ago to help the children and community there.

John would travel back to America to earn money by painting homes. My family always made sure to have him over to benefit his cause. As he would paint, I would sit and listen in amazement to his enchanting stories. Ever since he came into my eighth grade class to share his special story, I always used to tell my mom that one day I would visit him in Nicaragua. I didn't know how and I didn't know when, but I knew I would make it happen.

*I'm starting to realize how thick headed and determined I sounded.*

Over a decade later, that dream came true. I saw that a group of college students was looking for a few more people to go on a service trip there. I immediately signed up after I found out that

John's home was one of the host sites in Nicaragua. It was one of those moments where life seemed to make perfect sense, and my purpose was being fulfilled in the most incredible way.

One of the best ways to grow and learn about yourself is to spend your time helping others. It opens your eyes to a new perspective, to a whole new world (for all of you Disney fans out there, you're welcome for now getting the Aladdin song stuck in your head. Sing away, my friends!).

Something that stood out to me during my international service trips was people's simplicity and gratitude. I remember being in church in rural Nicaragua and a woman went on and on about how grateful she was for waking up that morning, for being alive, for the breath she takes. Our ability to breathe is automatic.

Many people wouldn't think to stop and be grateful for it. It is normally overlooked. We even take it for granted. If we wake up each morning with a grateful heart and eager mind, we can live that day to the fullest with the utmost gratitude. The possibilities are endless.

I grew as a person and teacher through my service experiences. I've taken that mindset and innate gratitude and applied it to my own daily life. Many times I feel misunderstood, but I don't let that shake me. I try to hold onto these core beliefs in my heart and encourage other people to shine light on those areas in themselves. Spend your time with people who *do* understand your passions and who share the same values as you do. It's that simplicity and gratitude for life that keeps you grounded.

There will be people who don't agree or understand your point of view. Accept that their life experiences led them to those limiting beliefs, and be brave enough to follow the intuition in your own heart. Some people didn't understand my desire to go on service trips because they lacked the ability to see from a perspective other than their own. Unfortunately, they tainted the preparation period prior to my trips with painful words rather than acceptance that this was something I felt called to do. They missed out on the full joy of some of the biggest experiences in my life because they chose to be narrow-minded and live in fear. As much as it hurt, I can't judge them for that. It's how they choose to live given the experiences they've been through.

In order to maintain my happiness and excitement, I silenced their negativity and knew in my heart that I was embarking on a life-enhancing experience. **My faith was greater than my fear.** I am grateful for living fearlessly and going after opportunities that helped me grow and inspire others along the way. Seeing and fully experiencing the way other people live gave me the greatest insight into poverty, living simply, and gratitude.

As a teacher in today's world, it is important to have an open mind to different perspectives of the world. Our students come to us with varying beliefs, values, and viewpoints. It's up to us to teach them to be understanding and empathetic toward other people's perspectives. Teach them that they don't have to always agree or be friends with everyone because that's not realistic, but they need to at least be respectful to everyone. **That lesson alone could change the world.**

## Tough Mudder Teachings

*Strength doesn't come from what you can do. It comes from overcoming the things you once thought you couldn't.*

—Rikki Rogers

As my husband and I embarked on yet another adventure with my first Tough Mudder Challenge, we read these following rules for our upcoming event consisting of twelve miles and twenty-five military style obstacles:

As a Tough Mudder I pledge that ...

- I understand that Tough Mudder is not a race but a challenge.

- I put teamwork and camaraderie before my course time.

- I do not whine—kids whine.

- I help my fellow mudders complete the course.

- I overcome all fears.

These rules have teaching written all over them. Teaching requires a certain strength that we must dig deep to uncover within ourselves; then we must believe in it once we have it in our grasp. Teaching is a challenge worth fighting for.

Teachers are quick to feel alone in the chaotic whirlwinds of all teaching entails. We often forget that we have support in our fellow colleagues. We are a team. One with the same ultimate goal of providing the best education for our students as well as focus on their well-being. We've all had days where our first reaction was to whine about things that were out of our control because sometimes it just feels good to whine it out and be the needy one for a change.

Instead, acknowledge that you don't agree with whatever the situation is and that it may take extra effort. Then work hard to adjust your mindset, so you can move forward successfully. I would, however, highly recommend the good kind of *wine*-ing during the school year. A little rest and RELAXation never hurt anybody, remember that. Teachers show teamwork by helping their fellow teacher friends achieve goals and complete the course of the school year.

We certainly overcome many fears. Every day brings about a new challenge, but we continue to grow along the way. If someone tells you that you can't do something because of their own fears and insecurities, look at them and declare, "Watch me." It's so satisfying.

## Mr. Superman

Brandon (I'd say you're on a first name basis with him by now) inspires me every single day in so many ways. Quickly captivated by his unique outlook on life, I knew my life would be better and more positive because of him. He has continued to prove this right since day one. He was diagnosed with type 1 diabetes when he was nine years old. This came as a surprise to him and his family.

Many parents in this situation would limit what their child is involved in after a diagnosis like this, but not his. They told him, "Diabetes doesn't define you. You define diabetes." Although it was a big adjustment in their daily lives learning how to remain healthy and manage his diabetes, he continued to be active and do the things he loved.

Not once in the many years of being with Brandon has he complained or talked negatively about having type 1 diabetes. Instead, he talks about how *grateful* he is for it. Yes, you read that correctly. Having this change in his life has made him realize how grateful he is for what he does have. He proudly claims that he is the healthiest he has ever been *because* of diabetes. If he didn't have diabetes, maybe he wouldn't be as mindful of what he eats and of his health.

One day, Brandon was in the middle of his usual routine involving needles, changing his injection site, and refilling the insulin into his pump. I flinch more than he does. I told him, "You're so brave."

He quickly responded, "I'm not brave. The men and women fighting for our country are brave. I just need to poke myself with needles a few times a day." His response left me in awe. Where did this man come from? And thank you, God, for sending him my way.

His outlook and ability to express gratitude for something others may view as a burden makes him freaking Superman in my eyes. Sometimes I find myself complaining if a part of my body aches or I'm curled over with cramps, but him? He fights for his life every day without complaint. No. Big. Deal. He makes me want to be better and is my daily reminder to put gratitude at the center of my focus.

Teachers have the ability to shape the minds of children. I can't help but wonder who helped shape Brandon's mind. It is truly extraordinary. What are you filling up your students' cute little minds with? Are you helping them focus on the good and *look beyond the clouds*? It is my sincere hope that you and everyone in your classroom express gratitude often and encourage it in good moments and bad.

Sometimes it is easy to focus on how noisy or messy your classroom is. Instead, be grateful for the noise. For it is proof that children are interacting, engaging in meaningful conversations, expressing ideas, and learning from one another. Be grateful for the mess. For it is proof that learning is taking place through exploration and dare I say ... *fun?*

At home, be grateful for laundry, dishes, cleaning, and chores like having to mow your lawn. It is proof that your family has clothes to wear, food to eat, a home to call your own, shelter on cold or rainy days, and land for your family to embrace the beauty and wonders of nature. If all people were to think in this way more often, life would seem brighter and more pleasing. Start by modeling gratitude for your class and for your family. That positivity will spread.

## Together, Knit and Woven

I student taught in a very small town in Pennsylvania. I gained the most beneficial experiences and reminders of what matters most in life from the children in my class. My journey to this school began one year prior. During one of my many observation assignments as a college student, I was graced with the honor of working with Ann in her first grade classroom.

She embodied the qualities you would imagine an angel to have. We clicked right away and worked so well together. She invited me to share my fresh perspective while she taught me about experiences she'd encountered during her many years of teaching. The following year, also her final year before retirement, she requested to have me as a student teacher. Gratitude filled my heart. I knew she would help continue shaping me into the teacher I was meant to become.

Ann and I were grateful to have such a strong bond because we needed to lean on each other often with handling the effects of our students' home lives. At least five new students were added to our class, but they each arrived without warning. They would show up at our classroom door on their first day, and we would need to quickly accommodate our new little munchkin, not knowing what challenges were ahead. Flexibility and teamwork were essential during these few months of constant change.

One little boy, let's call him Kyle, was expelled from the school he had transferred from because of his anger issues. We were nervous about how he would mix with our other emotionally draining students, rightfully so. One day he got in trouble during physical education class for falling asleep on the gym floor and not participating. The teacher was furious. I took him aside to get his side of the story, and he opened up more than I expected.

Kyle told me stories of how tired he was because his mom would hit him with a belt on his head if he didn't take care of his newborn brother overnight. This first grader was in charge of heating the baby bottle in the microwave and feeding the newborn while his mom slept through the night.

He was an intelligent boy who was dealing with the responsibilities of an adult ... at the age of seven. It was suddenly clear why he would act out or fall asleep in class. By taking the time to listen, create a bond with him, and build trust, Kyle had fewer and fewer outbursts of anger while in our class. He simply needed to be heard.

One girl, let's call her Adela, stopped coming to school for a few days straight with no notice or warning. The police were sent to her house to investigate, and they found an empty home. Adela returned a week later, explaining that she had to live with family in New York City for the week. That took a toll on her academically and emotionally.

Another little boy, let's call him Jimmy, was abused and evidently brainwashed by his father who then left him in his Grammy's care. Jimmy would say he knew his dad would come back for him. He never did. This precious child would be found hiding under desks banging his head against the tiled floor, wall, or the desk itself. Jimmy would harm himself during his continuous meltdowns to the point where we would find ourselves lying beside him talking him down from his ledge. Let me remind you, this was a general education class.

Then there was a girl named Ella. Ella was in her third foster home and not being treated well there. Her foster parent would lock her in a room for hours at a time and neglect Ella's basic needs. Ella required extra attention because of her drastic range of emotions due to an antidepressant she was taking. I was grateful that she immediately bonded with me. I learned so much from working with her.

One day when I walked the class to gym, they were telling me they would miss me ... in those *long* forty minutes away. I reassured them I would be back when gym was over, and before I left, many of them came over to hug me goodbye. As they sat down, Ella stayed by me and gave me an extra hug. She started to hum, so I joined her. She put her tiny hand in mine, so I started twirling her in a circle.

The brightest smile came on her face. I could see her drifting off into her imagination. For that moment, she was a ballerina performing in front of a sold-out venue. The audience was in awe of her poise and grace. On her face was pure joy. That happiness came from sharing the simplest moment together. It let Ella be a little girl for only a moment, so she could silence the heavy adult issues that surrounded her every single day.

It is in these little moments that gratitude fills my heart, and I put things into perspective. They help me focus on what actually matters in education. These children, your own students—*need you.* Care for them in a way that will make a lasting impression on their hearts and yours. Help them see the good in the world. Many times you're one of the few people in their life giving them a voice and unconditional love.

This precious little girl would tell me every day that she didn't want to go home after school and that she loved coming to school because she knew I would always be waiting there for her. I was one of the few people in her life who made her feel special, loved, and truly cared for.

My heart broke a few weeks later as Ella came to me crying and telling me that she was being sent to a new foster home. She would be leaving our class. Through her uncontrollable tears she begged me to never forget her. With tears streaming from my eyes, I responded, "How could I *ever* forget you, my sweet girl?"

Let this sink in for a moment while I catch my breath over here.

When missionary and best-selling author Katie Davis was twenty-two, she went on a service trip to Uganda and fell in love with the people there. She found herself staying and adopting thirteen girls while also improving the greater community. Needless to say, Katie Davis is a beautiful soul.

In her book *Kisses from Katie*, Katie Davis wrote: "The number of days or weeks we are together isn't important; what really matters is the way God knits our hearts together during the time He chooses for us to be in one another's lives. And that He would weave our stories together in such a powerful way."

Children are the teachers too if you let them be. I encourage you to share simple moments with your students and create deep bonds that you will cherish for years to come. The simplest acts of love and kindness are sometimes all it takes to make a difference in a child's life. These micro moments make the most immense impact on our hearts. It makes us want to be the best version of ourselves—for ourselves and for our students who look up to us so dearly.

In such a fast-paced world, we are quick to expect too much from each other, especially our children. We seem to forget that they are learning and growing each day, so they are bound to make mistakes from time to time. The academic rigor and expectations have changed drastically since I was in school. Remember to find gratitude in the simple moments and let these students be children!

**You are not only changing your students' lives. The children are changing yours.** You will become a better person and teacher because of them. Be aware of their feelings and situations at home that could affect their performance or focus at school. This is a higher priority than academics. We teach and care for the child as a whole—mentally, spiritually, emotionally, and physically.

The impact a teacher, mentor, leader, or parent can have on a child is the most significant influence in their life. They will take all the lessons they have learned from us with them on their journey through life. Most importantly, be grateful for the personal and classroom experiences you have had and for the lessons you've learned along the way. It has prepared you for where you are now. And for what is yet to come.

## Self-Reflect

- Reflect on a time when you accomplished something you set your mind to, with or without the support of others.
- List the colleagues and/or students you have encountered that made you grow as a teacher. What did they teach you?
- What qualities do you possess that a mentor or helpful colleague should have?
- What lessons have you learned from specific events in your personal and professional life?

## *Take Action*

- Thank a teacher friend you love working with and tell them how amazing they are!
- Help a fellow teacher in any way you can to have a more positive day, week, or year.
- Plan a short lesson about gratitude for your students. Help them become aware of moments of gratitude throughout each day by modeling it for them.
- Be grateful, always.

# 7. Jumping Into the Unknown

---

Take a moment to think about a time when you broke that endless cycle of feeling settled into your comfort zone and took a giant leap into the unknown. You truly felt alive and lived life to the fullest.

I encourage you to try something new, even if it terrifies you. **Be open to change. The more you resist it, the harder it will be to adjust.** When you challenge yourself and overcome fear, you learn a lot about yourself and life in the process. I've watched people in my life let fear control their daily existence. The result: they are unhappy and always counting down to retirement or another time that they'll finally be fully happy.

Think of an event that forced you to step out of your comfort zone and ended up being the greatest learning experience of your life. Keep one of my favorite quotes in mind. The poet Erin Hanson said, "What if I fall? Oh my darling, what if you *fly?*"

When you focus on the possibility of falling, you're letting fear take over. When you start focusing on the possibility of flying, you're setting yourself free. Free from limitations, fear, doubt, insecurity. Stepping into a world of new experiences, adventure, passion, possibility.

If you had no limitations—monetary or physical—what would you want to try? What dreams would you reach for? If I didn't choose to take a risk in the experiences that challenged me, I would have missed out on the greatest adventures of my life. What are you missing out on?

**Don't allow fear to stand between you and your awaited adventures.** Start by saying yes to something that scares you. I promise you it will be life changing and memorable and worth the risk. I would rather have tried and failed than not tried to "fly" at all. I hope you do the same.

## We Rise

It's not every day you see the word "jail" on a teacher's resume. Yet, it's on mine. Not in the way you might be thinking. When I was a sophomore in college, I was given a unique opportunity. One that required me to step out of my comfort zone.

A woman visited our college education class and explained how she volunteered with women in prison. She wrote with the incarcerated women and gave them a safe place to share their life stories and cope. She helped them see the good in themselves and reach for better days in the future.

This inspiring woman asked for volunteers to participate in a special program with her. She hoped to create a play combining the talent of seven education students with three former inmates. We were given little direction at first to see where sharing our own stories would lead us. What it led to was something absolutely incredible.

Over the next few months, we created, wrote, and performed a play titled "We Rise," raising awareness of women in prison, their childhoods, and how to identify signs of neglect and abuse in our future students.

I vividly remember our first meeting. We didn't know what to expect. As the women shared their lives with us, there wasn't a single dry eye in the room. We were so moved by their ability to keep fighting in the midst of so much pain and sorrow. We felt ourselves comparing childhood stories and identifying the vast differences we noticed.

In my childhood bedroom, you would find my parents reading me a bedtime story while tucking me in and singing lullabies. In theirs, you would see them getting abused physically or sexually, being sold for prostitution, hearing parents challenging them to take pills or drugs as fast as they could as if it were a race. This began at the age of five and was continual for them.

One woman described a time when her mother's boyfriend sold her on the street for prostitution and she was missing from school for five days. "How did my teachers not notice this?" she asked. This was when our ears perked up, and we put ourselves in that situation. What would we have done if that were our student?

In the time we spent together, we realized that although our paths and experiences may have been different, we each still had struggles and the desire to rise above. To *look beyond the clouds*. I learned the importance of being a voice for the voiceless and giving people—and students—a second chance.

"The kids who need the most love will ask for it in the most unloving ways." I keep this quote in my planner and in my desk as a reminder to look past the extreme behaviors being displayed in class. To figure out the reason why it is happening and how to best address their needs rather than yell at them for their desperate calls for attention. It sounds a lot easier said than done, but with a boatload of patience and compassion it is possible. Look for the warning signs and address them, so children who are struggling and in great need can be saved.

Being a voice for the voiceless causes teachers to stand up for those students or issues that they believe in. I've realized lately that many times we teachers are voiceless in our districts. Many decisions are made about what goes on in our classrooms without our voice and input. This can include the overwhelming amount of expectations, paperwork, and data collection in order to prove that we are capable teachers, which sets a stressful tone in a school.

Some schools are fortunate to have incredible administration who help teachers feel successful while other schools have the opposite. That *I'm gonna getcha* attitude makes teachers feel unappreciated and not trusted. Teachers are professionals and, may I add, miracle workers. Thus, we should be treated as such. We should be allowed the freedom and creativity to challenge ourselves in and out of the classroom.

As challenging as it is, don't let the distractions and expectations keep you from noticing and prioritizing helping those students in need. You can—and will—change lives. You've already been doing it for years, you super teacher you! **Despite our struggles, both personal and professional, we can all choose to rise.** Provide yourself and your students with a safe and loving environment, so they can thrive and rise above whatever challenges come their way. If their view is cloudy, help them *look beyond the clouds* and live in the sunshine.

Working with these women on this play taught me how to best support students with incarcerated parents. Keep the child engaged and interested in school. Encourage group activities, so they are not isolated. Develop a positive relationship with their new caregiver. Anticipate and accept difficult days. Support the child when they have the opportunity to communicate with their parent in prison. Always focus on the positive. Maintain high expectations so they strive to be their best. Monitor their behavior and academic progress. If possible, provide extra sets of clothing, food, and materials to help meet their basic needs.

In coming up with this list, I realized that all children would benefit from these gestures that teachers seem to do without second thought. Hence, this is why teachers, including you, are some of the most loving and incredible human beings on Earth. Call me dramatic, but I still believe it's true.

If I hadn't said yes to this opportunity, I would have never met these beautiful women and learned from them. I took a leap of faith and challenged myself even when I didn't know what to expect. The beauty of stepping out of your comfort zone is discovering the unknown and how it can impact your life in the greatest ways.

This concept can trickle down to our classrooms as well. If children are scared to try something new or freeze every time they see a math word problem, they'll never fully learn. We can teach them to be brave problem solvers as they face each given challenge with learned skills and strategies.

Explain to them that they will fail and make mistakes in life, but it is how they pick themselves up again that truly matters. Don't sugarcoat this for them, or else they won't be able to handle failure.

As a future member of society, children need to experience failure and know how to cope in a healthy way. Learning from our mistakes is one of the best hands-on ways to *learn*. Do they stay down and give up or do they get up, set a new goal, and work hard to achieve it? This, I've realized, is something that needs to be taught.

Each week when I share their weekly test scores with my students, I have them analyze what they did well in and where they can improve for next week. They set a goal for the following week. These simple skills of self-monitoring progress, setting goals, and taking responsibility for their success are essential for them to develop. As much as we wish we could sugarcoat failure for our children, it will only be detrimental to their future.

To every problem, there is a solution (depending on how hard we try). Many children today don't seem to think critically when presented with a problem. Adults tend to solve it for them because—heaven forbid—they struggle. We can't keep babying kids. What will happen when they turn into adults? They won't be able to work through a problem or be responsible or make choices on their own. They won't understand how to handle being held accountable for anything. Oh, sweet Jesus, we can't let this happen!

## The Five

The Beatles had the right idea all along. All you need is love. The question is *Are we giving love in the way people best receive it?* Everyone should read Gary Chapman's *The Five Love Languages*. It is the most insightful and beneficial book I have read. I enjoyed it so much that I also read his book, *The Five Love Languages for Children*.

I wish every brave soul preparing to be a teacher could read these books because it really opened my eyes and made sense. According to Chapman, the five love languages are (1) words of affirmation, (2) quality time, (3) receiving gifts, (4) acts of service, and (5) physical touch. This applies to adults and children.

As I was reading, I quickly thought of specific students and situations that apply to each love language and how best to address their individual needs. It's important to express love to each child in a way *they* understand it best. Just because you feel loved by receiving gifts, doesn't mean your child does. They may prefer quality time or hugs and snuggles.

Understanding your students' love languages can make all the difference in behavior management in your classroom. It helps them feel loved, safe, and cared for, ultimately allowing them to learn and reach their full potential.

If you don't identify a child's love language, you can cause emotional damage without meaning to. For example, if a child's love language is physical touch, they yearn for affection through hugs, kisses, cuddle time, etc. If a parent were to physically harm this child by hitting or shoving in some way, it causes the child to shut down completely and lose trust in that parent. That damage is then brought into the classroom making it extremely difficult for them to see past and cope with the trauma.

Reading Chapman's book, you may have some revelations of your own and come to understand yourself more too. I certainly did. I highly recommend you read and apply it to your own life and classroom. It will help you create a more understanding and compassionate learning environment (and home for your own children).

## Yes Time

Don't limit your options when interviewing for a teaching job. You never know where an unexpected opportunity may lead you. It's important to challenge yourself and step out of your comfort zone by being open to change in your district and classroom, but it's equally as important to do so during the interviewing process.

The interview process can make many people feel nervous, unprepared, and insecure usually because it is so incredibly important to do well that you don't want to "mess it up." In a world where we are given infinite opportunities for greatness and education beyond anything past generations were given, we still struggle with the ongoing fight of feeling not good enough. This can truly impact the way you treat yourself, interact with others, and live your life.

I've taken notice of the many teachers who have shut out potential opportunities by being too picky or specific in their ideal classroom while job hunting. While it's nice to have a dream scenario in mind, it can also be very limiting if you let it stop you.

When I was moving from New York to New Jersey, as mentioned I'd been teaching kindergarten in a Catholic school with the goal of switching over to the public school system. I sent out— are you ready for this?—application packets to fifty districts in New Jersey. *Twice.*

One during the winter when I knew I was definitely moving that coming June, then again in the spring during prime interview time. The packet included my cover letter, resume, letters of recommendation, and a colorful brochure detailing why I would be a good candidate for their district.

I sent them to the fifty districts near the area we would be moving to, in hopes of getting a job prior to the big move. I didn't even know if the districts had jobs available, but I sent them anyways. For exposure. So if a job came up, they would think back to that colorful brochure and give me a call.

Creating and sending these packets en masse challenged me because I had to push myself and be confident in my abilities to put myself out there on that scale. Shortly after, I heard from a district that others told me to be wary about. I didn't listen. I refused to be too picky. If anything, this would give me practice interviewing. I originally interviewed for a sixth grade position. No thank you! But *I went anyways.* I was open to change and challenging myself whatever the position may be.

It is difficult to find and secure a full-time teaching position in New York, New Jersey or anywhere for that matter, so I knew I had to be open to new ideas and experiences. The assistant super-intendent was one of my interviewers, and she acknowledged the jump I would be making from kindergarten to sixth grade. I told her it would be a challenge, but I was willing to do it and prove myself worthy.

The interview went very well, and I left feeling excited but also slightly terrified of being asked to teach the sixth grade. Subjects and topics started racing through my mind in math, science, social studies. What if I had to teach geography? What in the world was I getting myself into?

I believed if I was meant to teach in that district, I would find a way to make it all work as I took a leap of faith. I received a call from the assistant superintendent a few days later stating that they would like me to come back for a meeting with the superintendent. She hinted that this meant I was all set and about to be hired.

To my surprise, she informed me, "I know your experiences lend to the younger grades, so I did some thinking and switching around. How does third grade sound to you?" And there it was. All of the puzzle pieces falling perfectly into place.

That had always been my "ideal" grade that I dreamed of teaching. If I hadn't been open to new ideas or experiences, I don't know where I would have ended up ... possibly jobless. I didn't harp on the unknown. *I looked beyond it.*

Because of my openness and willingness to say yes, I found myself preparing to work in a Title 1 school that may seem challenging to others, but I looked at it as an opportunity to relive moments from my past international service trips. The children came from very difficult home lives, so I felt more like a counselor at times, but I knew I was exactly where I was meant to be. All because I said yes.

The district entailed more paperwork, data collection, and expectations from the teachers. Most of all, it required a certain warmth and patience to address the students' challenging lives and to present academics in a way where they could understand everything despite their past or ongoing traumas. Most of the children looked at me as their parent, their champion. I lived up to that expectation each day despite the emotional and physical toll it took on my body. They needed me. They needed that attention and love.

Every day we teach is stepping into the unknown and challenging ourselves. Yet, we continue on in those glimpses of appreciation and love from our students. My mom told me I would start drinking coffee my first year of teaching to help me through. Instead, I found wine. So when all else fails, treat yourself to a glass of whatever makes you smile and know that you are doing the very best you can. Tomorrow is a new day.

## The Ground Up

In the cold winter months I was grateful for shoveling my long driveway. Yes, you read that correctly. I was grateful for shoveling … snowstorm after snowstorm. You probably have never heard someone say that before, especially someone who wishes they could spend every day on the beach or someplace warm. Nevertheless, this is true for me since the very first time I shoveled my driveway at our first home.

It was after a long day of work and I wanted to do it before Brandon got home, so I could surprise him. It's the small things that count, right? As I shoveled the driveway I took the time to appreciate the beauty around me.

I noticed that the tips of the trees were lit up with a magnetic red from the sunset beyond the mountain. I realized how much I loved the look of trees lined with freshly fallen snow. Nature is remarkable. Nature is healing. Nature is that fresh breath of air or moment to simply "be" present. I wish those moments on everyone. So few take the time to notice.

It was a few short weeks after we moved in. However, our journey leading us to this first home was, well ..., unique, to say the least. A typical moving process consists of attending an open house, giving an offer, having it accepted, applying for a mortgage, packing what feels like hundreds of boxes, then fast-forward to moving day and off you go walking over that threshold for the first time. Pure bliss.

Our moving story is *slightly* different.

Sometimes life gives you unexpected opportunities, and it is up to you to choose if you are willing to challenge yourself and take that leap or not. We chose to leap. We took a chance that could have led to failure. But we knew it is in failure that you learn something new about yourself and a topic you may have never known, so there was nothing to lose. With our power team status, we began.

For a few months, my husband and I had been casually checking local listings for homes to get an idea of where we would want to move and raise a family once our apartment lease was up. One January morning, we came across what seemed to be a shell of a house abandoned in the midst of renovations. We were hoping for a fixer-upper, but this was beyond what we had imagined.

We managed to find the most run-down home around. It had no walls, floors, electricity, or plumbing, and was about to be knocked down—that is, until we decided it was our future castle. Don't be confused. It was a very tiny "castle," but it was *ours*.

Immediately, we channeled our inner Chip and Joanna Gaines and were ready to take on this challenge together. We began dreaming of the possibilities of this home. We emailed the real estate agent and received a phone call shortly. The agent was probably just relieved anyone was interested!

We met at the "house" that same day, and Brandon and I were hooked. Images of a new layout and decorating ideas swirled in my mind. I was more hesitant than Brandon was, rightfully so, but his constant reassurance that we could handle this as a team was what sold me. Plus, I could envision the final home, and that got me excited to create that charming vision.

Many people thought we were insane because, well, we were. Yet, I admired my husband's ability to disregard other people's negative input and move forward with confidence towards our vision. We silenced the negativity, visualized our breathtaking view, and *looked beyond the clouds* with hope in our hearts. We finally closed on the sort-of home on May 18, 2017, then went straight from there to start working.

We began the six-month process by demoing the horribly completed framing and subflooring in the empty shell. We spent multiple hours working and changing the entire layout of the home. We did everything from months of demo, fully insulating the crawl space, waterproofing the house from the inside out by digging a trench around the whole house for a french drain, and covering the inside walls with tar, cutting and installing innumerable two-by-fours for the framing, balancing on the floor beams until we installed the subflooring a few months in, finishing touches, and numerous inspections along the way.

I learned the name and use of every construction tool under the sun. My personal favorite was the chop saw. Brandon would yell the measurements, I would cut each two-by-four (and write a little love note or our wedding song lyrics on it), then he would install them. We worked for a ton of hours after work and all weekend long. Pure exhaustion and perseverance turned into pride and amazement, which kept us going. We would stand in awe upon completing each step, admiring the hard work it took to get there.

**There were so many moments that I would snap out of the rhythm we were in and realize the magnitude of what we were accomplishing.** I would've never believed anyone if they'd told me this was something I would tackle. But it was. All because I said yes to a challenge. Yes to a dream that *we* made come true.

If you visit my site—www.lookbeyondtheclouds.com—you'll find before-and-after pictures of the house as well as pictures of Brandon and me building it out at various stages.

~

It's interesting how teachers teach children to have courage, believe in themselves, set goals, and never give up. Yet, we seem to forget that those "rules" apply to our own lives as well. Practice what you preach, my friend! You deserve it! I regularly share examples from my own life of when I had to be brave, step out of my comfort zone, persevere, and so on, with my students—like my house-building experience.

Many times children think their teacher is on a pedestal and perfect, never making mistakes. These stories about our own lives show them that we are human and imperfect, but trying our best every single day, just like we ask of them. Teach your students (and yourself!) to have courage, try something new, challenge themselves. Assure them that it's expected to feel nervous in the process, but continue to persevere. Push through it. Let that little worry act as motivation to keep trying. If you believe you can, you will certainly go far.

Dreaming big, perseverance, and more perseverance—that's what makes you stand out in this ever-evolving world. Explore your strengths and weaknesses. Learn how to use your strengths to add value to your life and other people's lives while also understanding how to work through your weaknesses in times of need. And be sure to teach your students the same.

When we step out of our comfort zone and into the unknown, this is when we learn who we really are and what we are capable of.

# Self-Reflect

- If you had no limitations—monetary or physical—what would you want to try? What dreams would you reach for?
- What limiting beliefs do you have that cause you to miss out on given opportunities? Do you allow fear to stand between you and your intended adventures? Shake the fear.
- When is the last time you have stepped out of your comfort zone in your home life and also your school life? Tried something new? Challenged yourself? How did it make you feel?
- Think of a time you let fear of *falling* take over and keep you from *flying*. What will you do next time to make sure you allow yourself the chance to fly?
- Which love language fits you best? How can you incorporate the five love languages into your life at home? At work?
- Change is inevitable in teaching. When was a time you chose to be open to change by saying yes to a new opportunity at work?

# *Take Action*

- Be open to change.
- Try something new.
- Don't allow fear to stand between you and your awaited adventures.
- Despite your struggles, have the desire to rise above and *look beyond the clouds*.
- Determine the love languages of your students, so you can best meet their needs.
- Encourage your students to try something new and report back with what they learned from the experience.

# 8. Lighting Your World

How often do you give people your full attention? In the social media-infused, fast-paced world we live in it is rare that we put our cell phones down and truly listen to someone. You know, the old-fashioned way ... face-to-face. I often joke that I was born in the wrong time period because, while technology is wonderful and provides us with fascinating exposure to the world, it can be so detrimental to our relationships and interactions with other people if we allow it to be.

This issue is also evident in the classroom. Teachers are presented the near-impossible challenge of teaching children basic social skills while also trying to maintain their attention by competing with the instant gratification world of technology to simply teach our math or reading lesson for the day. Children are used to constant stimulation, so they lack the ability to pause for a minute in between lessons and typically blurt out, "What are we doing next?"

When I was younger, the world of teaching and education looked vastly different. We followed directions, listened to lessons (for the most part), interacted with classmates, never dared to question a teacher, but most notably, we understood the word *patience*. Now children seem to feel entitled to question authority and lack the understanding of how to be patient and wait their turn. I ponder where and when this drastic shift took place. It is my hope that parents and teachers can get a grasp on how to end this spiraling trend.

Sometimes we assume that children are learning these basic concepts at home even to the smallest degree, but I've been proven wrong with this assumption many times. You know what they say about making assumptions. Children don't engage in enough meaningful conversation at home as often as they should. Instead, they're wrapped up in the isolating world of technology.

This seems evident in many families today. However, most of my current students come from bilingual families and the challenge with that is their parents often work several jobs, so they are rarely home at the same time as their children. Even if they are, some of my students don't know Spanish and their parents don't know English. This baffles me.

Who is engaging the child in conversations at home? How do they communicate effectively with this lack of quality time and a potential language barrier? These are things you don't expect or think of when you are studying to be a teacher. Yet, they impact the overall learning environment in your classroom each day.

I once saw a slideshow consisting of people on their cell phones who were all in the same room together. The startling part was the cell phones were erased from the photos so all that was left was the lack of face-to-face interaction and the zombie-like state people delve into while on their technology.

Instead of seeking approval from within or from the closest people in our life, we find ourselves basing our self-worth on how many "likes" or "comments" we get on a picture we uploaded to social media. Instead of comparing your life to the filtered-version of someone else's life, create real-life memories of your own with those you love.

I may be part of a select few at this point, but I print all of my photos and put them into photo albums. No, not the ones online where I can share it with thousands of people with the click of a button. The kind that sits on the bookshelf in our living room. For our family and close friends' eyes only. Crazy concept, I know. Of course it's fun to share some memories in a more public way (for instance, providing a few visuals for you as you read through this book!), but there's something so personal and intimate about people not having to know every detail of your life.

## Showing Up

The best gift you can give someone is the gift of your time and your full attention during whatever amount of time you are able to give. I like to call this the "power of presence, not presents." Time is a strange concept. Life is hectic and time seems to slip by all too quickly. Everyone wishes they could *have more time* to do the things they want to do or accomplish the dreams they would do if they *had the time*.

But when given the time, they don't always use it wisely. Therefore, the problem isn't about *finding the time*. You already have it! It's about prioritizing what you do in that given time.

What truly matters to you? What is getting your energy's full attention? Your goals? People? Technology? Be willing to make sacrifices for the things that are *worth your time*. It will enhance the quality of your life. Make sure your cell phone isn't a higher priority than face-to-face human connection.

During my service trip to Jamaica, I was inspired to be a light for other people and hopeful to inspire others to do the same. One day our group leader, Tom, explained how a child taught him to "show up" for other people in life.

So often we find ourselves not being fully present in the moment and giving people the time they deserve from us because we're too busy or we're going over our super lengthy to-do list in our head. This can strain our relationships over time.

If you don't take the time to really listen and show the other person that what they say and do matters to you, then they will stop coming to you for support. If you feel your mind wandering while someone is speaking to you, take control and change the focus in your mind. Come back to the present moment.

With an open heart and an open mind, actively remind yourself to "show up" for the people in your life, whether it's for family members, friends, students, or colleagues. **We, as human beings, have the desire to be heard, loved, and accepted.** By spending time with someone you care about you are fulfilling that desire.

On this trip, I met a young boy named Jamar, who was visiting a family member at the nursing home we spent time at. We played hide-and-go-seek because that game is awesome and will never get old. I will always remember the brightest smile on Jamar's face and the joyful bellowing of his laughter.

When we played, Jamar didn't wait for me to find where he was hiding, so technically he was horrible at the game. He would run out and say in a squeaky little voice, "I'm right here!" I saw God in this little boy. God doesn't wait for us to find Him. He gives us signs and makes His presence known to us. All we need to do is open our eyes to it. This made me ponder the notion of "showing up" for someone. How can we make our presence known to others?

Apply this simple phrase to your everyday life. *Show up* for your colleague by noticing when they feel overwhelmed and offering a helping hand. *Show up* for your student when they want to tell you a story, even if it goes on forever with no point at all.

*Show up* for an old friend you lost touch with. *Show up* for your parents by calling them for no other reason than to see how they are. *Show up* for a sibling, grandparent, aunt, or uncle. *Show up* for a neighbor who needs help bringing the garbage pails to and from the end of their driveway. *Show up* for the poor and voiceless. **Show up and be the light in someone's life. Be the reason they smile that day.**

## Your Candle

Everyone has a light within them that can do one of two things. **It can shine for all to see and brighten the lives of those around them, or it can remain dim.** This light represents love, compassion, and our character. We have the ability to choose what we do with this light and essentially the life we want to live. Every decision we make will determine where our path will lead. Many people may not realize the immense impact their choices have on the course of their life.

My favorite line in Kathy Troccoli's song "Go Light Your World" is this: "Take your candle and go light your world." I listened to this song almost daily in preparation for my service trips because the message was so alluring of spreading your light and kindness to others. While finishing up my journaling one night in Jamaica, I heard a song playing in the distance. It got louder and I was speechless as I realized what song it was.

The inspiring song I had been listening to on repeat preparing my heart for our trip was suddenly playing in a passing car on the streets of Kingston, Jamaica! What were the chances of it playing in our exact neighborhood so many miles away from home? What an overwhelmingly powerful moment. We are all connected. The light in our hearts is bright and waiting to be shared with the world.

Spread your light and bring hope and happiness to others this week.

During my service trip to Nicaragua, I made the deepest connection with the group of glorious souls I traveled with. I didn't know any of them prior to going on the trip beyond a small introduction gathering. It's amazing what you can learn about people when all distractions are put aside, and you spend hours talking under a perfect nighttime sky full of twinkling stars.

From finding comfort in each other while in an unfamiliar living situation to facing fears together, whether it be walking to the latrine, i.e., hole in the ground, to use the bathroom in the blackness of the night or fighting off scorpions while moving bricks to build a home for a deserving local family. From taking turns filling up a small bucket from the water well to pour over each other's heads, considering that our shower ... you quickly learn about people and create deep connections with them through these unfamiliar yet incredibly humbling experiences.

During the duration of our trip, we did something called the guardian angel activity. On the first day of the trip, we were given a name of someone in the group. Our job was to look after them throughout the trip without them finding out who their guardian angel was. If they seemed to need support or someone to talk to or laugh with, we would *show up* and spend time with them to address whatever it was that they needed.

Toward the end of the trip, we revealed who we had been looking after. We lay on our cots and used string to connect ourselves to one another, creating a wondrous visual web of support and encouragement. It represented how all of us were connected that week with a single goal in mind. We each spoke about one another by complimenting them, sharing what we learned about them, listing their strengths, and how they inspired us.

If you are looking for a way to enhance the relationships among the staff in your school or the students in your classroom and create meaningful connections, this activity would be well worth your time. At the beginning of the week, you can give a name to the staff members or students, and encourage them to *show up* for that person. To help them when they seem upset or overwhelmed. To celebrate their victories, whether big or small. To be a listening ear and someone they can rely on.

**If you need a better support system at work, start by being one for someone else.** They will then feel inspired to help another person who will go help another. Start the chain reaction of support, encouragement, positivity, a helping hand, a listening ear, a shoulder to lean on. Okay, enough with all of the body part references. You get my point.

To put it simply, let's be one another's biggest fans and support each other through it all, aka be awesome for someone else and that awesomeness will return to you. Teaching challenges you each day, and sometimes you can't do it alone. Remember that it's okay to feel this way and seek help when you need it.

During one of those years that felt like I was running on a treadmill that was going too fast while forty people tossed balls at me yelling, "Catch!" all at once one of my colleagues reached out to me when I had really hit rock bottom with my class and sanity. I had made it all the way to April at that point, and the physical and mental exhaustion was real. I got to work one morning, put my things away, and sat at my desk to start my morning routine of preparing for the day. On my desk sat a note with a gift bag next to it. The note read:

*Michelle,*

*You're doing an amazing job. We know you're tired and worn down but you're making a difference. We have May and June left—you can do it!*

It wasn't signed, but I could tell who wrote it by their handwriting. Just another fancy skill we teachers have, right? In the gift bag was a reusable water bottle that I am actually using while I write this sentence. It is covered with positive words and character traits that describe what it means to be the best teacher.

This simple gesture healed my heart a bit more that day. It reminded me that I was not alone in my struggle and that all of the energy spent on this group of students was making a difference even if I struggled to see *beyond the clouds* and the daily exhaustion.

Relate to one another's struggles and understand them. Reach out to colleagues when they are having a bad day or when they have fabulous news to celebrate. If you love working with someone, tell them often. Write a simple card to show your appreciation.

I had a meaningful conversation about teaching, clouded views, and life with the art teacher at my first school, and the next day, I had a card in my mailbox from her saying how much she enjoyed our talk. I still keep in touch with her to this day. I've done this for many other colleagues to help light our world a bit more each day. Simple, kind gestures help you realize you are not alone.

In my current school, I have a few colleagues who I nearly consider family at this point. We have been through a lot, both personally and at work, and we've always leaned on each other. We let one another vent it out, then do our best to come up with solutions together of how to address the issue or handle it if it's out of our control.

When all else fails, we share a good laugh and remind one another what really matters. Everyone is facing a battle you may not know about, so take the time to reach out and embrace the power of human connection.

## Letting Serenity Reign

Imagine a place where you feel fully calm, serene, and at peace. It can be anywhere in the world! It may be at a beach or lake, watching a sunrise or sunset, spending time with a loved one, lying in a hammock, hiking up a mountain (or volcano), or a special chair in your home that you love to sink into while wrapped in the softest blanket. It can even be in the arms of someone you love.

Think of this place in your mind. Visualize every detail. What does it look like? What does it sound like? Create a vivid picture in your head of this special place.

What about this place makes you feel calm? Is it the quiet atmosphere or the sounds of nature, such as birds chirping or the ocean waves crashing on the shore? Is it the company of certain people that bring you the most peace? Is it the sound of a particular instrument or the physical feeling of a specific comfortable chair?

Now consider how we can work together to make our world a place where each individual feels this peace and joy. What actions can you do daily to help create this calm and peaceful environment whether you are at home, in your classroom, or anywhere? If people felt more encouraged, supported, cared for, happy, and so on, they would find more hope in each day, as well as more compassion for others. A parent more or less pointed to this very concept when, in the midst of the heightened tension from the upper administration in my district, she told my colleagues, "A person who feels appreciated will always do more than is expected."

Human beings have the power within to create a positive day for themselves and others by considering this concept and applying it throughout the day. Greeting people in the morning, giving genuine compliments, listening to someone in need, helping others see the good in humanity by being an example of it—all of these simple gestures can make the greatest impact in our day. **When you help other people, a satisfaction comes over you and boosts your own mood.**

Three places come to my mind when I consider this myself. The first place where I feel most at peace is curled up with my husband, baby boy, and our puppy. As corny as that sounds it is the absolute truth! Their calm demeanor and loving presence helps me pause and feel so at peace regardless of what my day was like.

The second place where I felt calm was during my service trip to Nicaragua. We were lying on a hammock looking at a star-filled sky. There is something about a starry night that captivates my attention and leaves me in awe of God's creations.

In that moment, I felt so calm and hopeful. I felt restored and healed of the chaotic daily life we seem to live. We all need a break sometimes to breathe and appreciate the beauty around us. I promised myself I would get a hammock, so I could bring myself back to that moment when I rock back and forth. As expected, my hammock is now easily my favorite part of our backyard.

The third place I feel most calm is watching a sunrise or sunset. Each morning as I eat breakfast, I watch the sunrise from my window and feel the serenity wash over me. The colors and sun poking through clouds create some of God's most stunning scenes. It serves as a reminder to *look beyond the clouds* toward the brightest sunshine no matter what you may face that day.

Now let's apply this peaceful-place idea to our classrooms.

In order to create a classroom that goes beyond academics and establishes a needs-fulfilling environment, we must build meaningful relationships with each student and learn about their individual needs. Our goal is to help meet the needs of our students and express an innate care for their well-being. We set the tone in the beginning of the school year for our students.

What better way to set the tone than by establishing the rules and expectations of our classroom together? Ask the students to close their eyes and think of their favorite place and how it makes them feel. A vivid image will come to their minds. For example, the beach because it is stress-free and fun or their bedroom because it is quiet and cozy. Once each student has shared their favorite place with the class, create a chart and fill in the students' responses. Highlight the words they used to describe it.

Explain that this is the kind of place we want our classroom to be. These are the feelings we want our classmates to have when they are in our classroom this year. This activity helps children visualize and describe what their ideal classroom would look like and what we need to do in order to make it that way. It promotes that positive and needs-fulfilling learning environment we desire.

Next, guide your class through the following my job/your job activity. Record responses to the following questions in a chart: What is my job as a student? What is not my job as a student? What is your job as a teacher? What is not your job as a teacher? Enable students to understand the role and responsibilities of the teacher and themselves. Refer to this chart often to create positive habits among the students.

Here are a few ideas to help get you started:

## My Job / Your Job

| Student's Job | Teacher's Job |
|---|---|
| * Complete my work | * Teach students all subjects |
| * Listen when others are speaking | * Correct student work |
| * Follow expectations and procedures | * Give consequences when needed |
| * Be a problem solver | * Make lesson plans |
| * Be helpful and kind | * Give helpful feedback |
| * Be respectful | * Be respectful |
| * Be responsible | * Be responsible |
| * Clean up after myself | * Get materials ready for the day |
| * Always do my best | * Always do my best |
| * Set goals and work hard | * Set goals and work hard |
| * Have fun | * Make learning fun |

| Not A Student's Job | Not A Teacher's Job |
|---|---|
| * Tattle on others | * Complete work for students |
| * Worry about what someone else is doing wrong | * Give answers on a test |

Lastly, come up with a list of class promises to use as classroom rules based on the brainstorming that took place. **When you create classroom expectations with your students and come up with why each one is important, they are more likely to follow them on a daily basis.**

They will monitor their own behavior and be motivated to engage in positive behaviors. Have students sign your class promise and display it in your classroom. The visual and daily reminder will help maintain the positive learning environment you and your students dream of.

Here is a sample Class Promise to help get you started:

**Our Class Promise**

* Support and love each other like a family
* Make good choices
* Be a leader
* Always do your best
* Be kind and polite to everyone
* Be willing to help others
* Be honest
* Be safe
* Listen when someone is speaking
* Persevere—never give up
* Follow directions the first time they are given
* Be respectful and responsible
* Have good manners
* Use walking feet in the classroom
* Keep learning fun!

## Joining the Chain

You get more of what you focus on. If you focus on yelling at the child who isn't listening, it is still a form of attention in their eyes, so they may continue that behavior. Some children think any attention is better than none. **If you focus on the good and**

**positive behaviors, more students will strive to be recognized for such behaviors.**

One way to encourage continued positive interactions is to create an ongoing class kindness chain. Set up a station in your classroom that has pencils and strips of colorful construction paper. Each time your students witness or are part of an act of kindness have them write it on the strip of paper. At the end of each day, read aloud the acts of kindness recorded on the papers and add them to the ongoing paper chain.

Once the chain is long enough, hang it up and decorate your classroom with these inspiring kind acts that your students helped create. This visual reminder of kindness helps strengthen the power of human connection in your classroom and instills in students the desire to be kind and loving people.

**When we display and celebrate the acts of kindness in our classrooms and personal lives, the world becomes a more beautiful place.**

Another way to build meaningful connections and relationships in your classroom is by asking your students to anonymously write one compliment about each of their classmates. At the end of the activity, each child will have at least twenty kind comments or memories to read about themselves.

Instantly, their little love tank will fill up. Their need for love, acceptance, and a sense of belonging will be satisfied. They will feel cared for and important. There is good in everyone. We just need to challenge ourselves to recognize it and make a point to recognize them for it, which will encourage them to continue that positive behavior.

These concepts seem mostly geared toward children, but in helping children learn these kind habits you are making your job as a teacher more enjoyable. You could apply these visuals among the staff in your school as well.

In the faculty room, you can have a board where everyone records shout-outs to other teachers to recognize successes and kind acts—big or small. You can have a wall of positivity and encourage teachers to post pictures that will inspire positivity and joy while they are eating their lunch.

On a more personal note, you can keep a journal and jot down kind acts that were done for you and ones you did for others. Reflect on how each one made you feel and how you can continue this trend each week.

~

Human beings yearn for love, acceptance, and a sense of belonging. Even people who are very outgoing can experience intense loneliness. I certainly have. This struggle continued at various points in my life, but it's made me the teacher I am today.

In elementary school, I attended a Catholic school with about forty students in my grade. I was very close with three girls and friendly with a different group of girls. Naturally I thought, *Why can't we all be friends?* So I brought the two small groups together, and they quickly decided that I got the boot. I wasn't "good enough" to be friends with them. They would draw pictures of me pointing out my "ugly" features, write notes, and talk and laugh about me when I was only a few feet away.

To add fuel to the fire, I would be made fun of for standing up for other peers in our class who were considered different or unpopular according to this girl group's superficial standards. (I question anyone's morals if they choose to name themselves the Tacky Ten.) If someone were sitting alone at lunch, I would be the first person to sit with them because I knew how it felt. On the other hand, they would resemble the scene from *Mean Girls* with catty girls squealing, "You can't sit with us!"

The intense feeling of loneliness and humiliation set into my heart at this early age and stayed for quite some time, resulting in a strong negative impact on my self-esteem. I struggled with not fitting in and exclusion for too long, but it taught me at a young age to never make someone else feel the way I felt in those dark, cloudy moments. I knew I was better off without them in my life, but it didn't necessarily ease the pain.

It's interesting to me now how I found comfort in teachers over the years knowing I wanted to become one myself. They saw my pain and took me under their wing, protecting my heart as much as they could. Three in particular from elementary school were angels sent down from Heaven!

They modeled for me the kind of teacher I wanted to become. They would let me help them grade papers or talk with me during recess, which was something I looked forward to. I don't know if I was mature for my age or if it was my unique outlook on life, but something always seemed to set me apart.

I would lose interest quickly at the first sight of drama among girls. I refused to put up with nonsense from girls who thought they were better than everyone in the world. I would rather be alone than with "friends" who weren't good and kind people.

In high school, the pattern shifted slightly, but the same loneliness remained. This time, I was friendly with many people, but lacked those solid friendships that I've heard could last a lifetime. Everyone lived far away from each other making it difficult to spend time together on the weekends. I felt overprotected by my parents like many teenagers do, so I didn't bother asking to go to friends' houses. I knew it would turn into the game of twenty questions, quickly making it frustrating and not worth the effort.

This impacted the friendships I did have. If peers keep asking for you to hang out but you keep saying no, they eventually stop including you. Instead, I babysat nearly every weekend in high school. This filled that void ever so slightly allowing me to dream of being a mother and teacher one day.

I learned at a young age to focus on the positive people in my life. These teachers showed me such love and compassion. They shed the brightest light for me to see through the darkness I felt in my heart. I honor them by doing the same for my students and other people every day of my life.

Bring the power of human connection into your classroom by connecting with students who seem lonely and help make them feel worthy, safe, and loved. You may be the first person who actually has taken the time to show them their worth.

A powerful activity you can do with your class that will make the greatest impact on understanding how our words and actions affect other people is called the hurting heart activity. Here it goes!

Have your class sit in a circle and get comfortable because why not? The first part of this activity begins with a tube of toothpaste and an empty plate. Hold the tube in your hand and let their minds wonder what in the world it could be for. Squeeze some of the toothpaste onto the plate. Ask your students if it is possible to put it back into the tube. You can even have a volunteer try to fit it all back in. This could get messy, but that just means they are exploring and learning is taking place!

Explain that this represents how once you say mean words you can't take them back. That's why it is so important to think before you say something hurtful. Encourage them to take a moment to think of something they have said to someone else that they wish they could take back. How did they feel after saying it? What did they do to try to make up for the hurtful words?

The second part of this activity is when they learn the meaning of the "hurting heart." Ask students to close their eyes and think about a time they were treated in a hurtful way. It can be recent or it can be from years ago. I usually share a story from when I was in middle school and a group of girls passed a note to each other that had a picture of me pointing out my ugly features. Big eyebrows, big curly hair, and braces. I say, "Isn't it crazy that I remember that drawing and how I felt so clearly even though it happened so many years ago?"

This part of the activity may spark many upsetting memories for some students. Tears will probably be shed. In this case, acknowledge that they have every right to feel upset by hurtful memories. Maintain a respectful tone by saying something like, "I appreciate how you are being respectful of how each other is feeling. It's ok to feel upset and cry. That happens to me too when I think of hurtful memories."

As the students think about an example from their own life, tell them to acknowledge each experience that comes to their mind and choose one example to focus on. Hand out a large heart made out of construction paper to each student. If they are at an age where they can write the memory on the heart, encourage that. If not, they can draw a picture.

Give your students the option of sharing their story to the class if they feel comfortable doing so. Many of them enjoy sharing their story. It helps them feel heard and supported. Once they are finished sharing, prompt the class to crumble their paper hearts into a ball. This represents how it was hurt. Have fun with this part.

Have them to squash it as tightly as they can without ripping it or stomp on it. Get those healthy coping strategies for anger in action! Those tears will turn to laughter at this point. They love being allowed to go crazy and destroy it. It makes them feel good to show that memory who's boss! After a minute of this, you'll need to reign them in a bit.

Next, tell your students to reopen their crumbled heart and try to smooth the wrinkles out as best as they can. This visual and exercise will help the children realize that like the wrinkles in their paper hearts, sometimes hurtful words never fully go away. We may be able to forget about them, but the damage is still there. Words and actions have lasting effects on other people.

Encourage them to be mindful of their words and actions toward other people. You don't want to cause a wrinkle on someone else's heart. Keep a sample of this hanging in the front of your classroom as a reminder of this lesson. The students will refer back to the wrinkled heart when issues arise and hurtful interactions take place.

Loneliness can greatly impact a person's well-being and mental health. It can cause people to seek acceptance or attention in ways they typically would stray away from. In knowing this, implement these strategies to promote the loving and productive learning environment you strive to achieve. Remember that a movement starts with one person. Let it be you. These children are worth it. *You* are worth it.

## Self-Reflect

- How often do you give people your full attention?
- How do you prioritize what you do with the time you are given each day?
- What is getting your energy's full attention? Your family? Your students? Technology? Your goals?
- Where do you feel fully calm and at peace? What does it look like? What does it sound like?
- Think of a time when you felt lonely. Who helped you see the light and *look beyond the clouds*?

# Take Action

- If you feel your mind wandering while someone is speaking to you, take control and change the focus in your mind. Come back to the present moment.

- Actively remind yourself to "show up" for the people in your life.

- Write a card to show your appreciation for someone at home and at work.

- Help someone today and watch how it boosts your mood and theirs.

- Complete the following activities with your class: ideal classroom, my job/your job activity, a class promise, class kindness chain, anonymous compliments list, and hurting heart activity.

- Praise positive behavior displayed in your class, so other children strive to be recognized for similar behavior.

- Reach out to students who seem lonely in your class. Help them feel worthy, safe, and loved.

# 9. Mastering Self-Love

T his chapter is a gift for you. Put your worries at ease as you read about the power and healing that comes from self-love. Take a much-needed break from your teaching worries and focus on the fabulous you.

**Focus on the incredibly amazing person you are and celebrate your journey to finding self-love—wherever you are in the process.** Then bring that love and confidence back with you to your classroom and see the effects it has on your teaching and overall *beyond-the-clouds* outlook.

Loving yourself starts with respecting yourself and thinking of yourself in a positive way. We spend minutes, hours, sometimes even days building up and encouraging our students and our own children at home. Telling them how proud we are of them, how wonderful and talented they are, how it's okay to make mistakes, teaching them how to get back up when they have failed.

**How often do you build yourself up?** Let that question sink in for a moment. Do you spend your precious time building yourself up with kind words and positive thoughts, or do you compare yourself to others resulting in a harsh tone? As you look in the mirror, do your small imperfections scream out at you, making themselves known? Or do you see the beauty that you are?

Take a moment and look in a mirror right now. Go on, I can wait. Focus only on your eyes. Your mind will quickly remind you of all of your imperfections trying to distract you. Acknowledge each thought as it drifts by; then silence it. Bring your focus back to your eyes. Look at the exquisite color; then prepare to look deeper. Eyes are like windows to a person's soul. To their past, present, and future.

Your eyes have witnessed moments of deep sorrow and darkness, but they have also witnessed moments of pure joy and light. Moments where *you looked beyond the clouds* and lived in that warm sunshine. Every memory from the past has shaped you into the person you are today and allows you to look toward a brighter tomorrow.

**If you look closely enough, you will find acceptance for the past, peace for the present, and hope for the future.** This is the first step to truly loving yourself.

During college, I was fortunate to have countless opportunities to spend weekends away at our university's retreat center at a stunning lake approximately thirty minutes from campus. I first heard about the lake house during orientation weekend and I was hooked. I signed up for my first retreat and fell in love with the scenery, the company, the healing, and the peace there.

Each retreat weekend consisted of an overall theme with the leaders sharing their life experiences in the most vulnerable way on specific topics. We would be assigned a small group that we would meet with after each talk to reflect and open up about our own lives. We shared our struggles, triumphs, and life experiences in such raw and honest ways. People thrive when they can relate to someone else's life story and connect in ways that heal a shattered heart.

Music was a big part of these retreats, and I'd always leave with new songs I could listen to when I needed inspiration to keep moving forward. We would gather as mostly strangers on Friday night and quickly turn into family by Sunday afternoon. There's that power of human connection again!

These special "get-away" weekends were the perfect escape from our hectic daily lives. There was something so powerful about taking time to focus on ourselves and allow growth to happen from the inspiration of other people. I found healing from past experiences, which would then turn into self-love and admiration of strength. Being able to overcome obstacles in life comes from a strong foundation of self-love.

Today's society seems to strip away our self-love and confidence from a young age, and many times we never quite seem to get it back fully. Unless, that is, if you work like hell to cleanse your brain of the constant brainwashing that takes place from other people and the media.

**Self-love emerges when you are capable of being self-aware.** Be mindful of your strengths and talents. Put them to good use. Celebrate them. Believe you are a freaking superstar because *you are*! I don't even need to know you to know that about you. If you're reading this book and have that desire to make your situation better, then that makes you a superstar in my eyes. Anyone who wants to better themselves and learn every day is that much closer to experiencing self-love to its fullest.

Be mindful of your weaknesses. Accept that they are something you need to work on. Will it take time to improve? Absolutely! That's where our skills of hard work, determination, and patience come in. It'll be worth your energy and perseverance.

**How you treat yourself is how others will treat you. You set the tone.** Maybe you learned this the hard way in your teenage years like I did. If you allow other people to control your mindset and bring you down with their negative view, they will. If you allow people to be disrespectful to you, they'll cut you with hurtful words in attempts of making themselves feel better. If you allow people to use you, they'll use away, reaping the benefits like a thief in the night.

As I've mentioned earlier, living in a home where we found ourselves walking around on eggshells to avoid outbursts after tragedy hit, I yearned for love and attention in ways I am not fond of. My self-love was fatally low causing me to frantically fill the missing void in my heart. I was broken. I know I'm not the only one who has let people use and disrespect them. Remember that self-love comes from self-acceptance and lessons learned. I wrote the following poem at the end of high school after I became self-aware of the way I was letting people treat me. I hope it can heal a part of your soul like it did for mine.

## Used

*Have you ever felt used?*
*You go through the motions feeling so empty inside*
*Your eyes begin to tear as your heart cries and cries*

*At night you curl up on your bed*
*And can't breathe from crying so hard*
*You try to catch your breath*
*Then wonder if it would even be worth it*
*Because you know the next time,*
*Things would all go the same way*

*You look in the mirror at a girl looking back at you*
*With tears streaming down her face*
*Is this really me?*
*What has all of this come to?*
*"God, give me a sign that things will turn around*

*And somehow be okay.*
*I need help and your strength.*
*For this, I pray."*

*Crying and crying until your stomach churns*
*When will this feeling ever go away?*
*I feel empty*
*I feel broken*
*I feel like my heart is bruised*
*I feel useless*
*I feel numb*
*This is what it feels like to be used*

*What a mess this has become*
*Will I ever have the strength to end this?*

*This isn't what it should be like*
*This isn't love in any range*
*So get out as soon as you can*
*Run far away until you can't anymore*
*To save yourself from heartache*
*And to redeem your precious soul*

*I yearn for happiness to fill my heart*
*But instead I have settled for this*
*And let them overpower me*
*This is what I deeply and truly regret*

*One day when I finally had enough*
*And couldn't take the pain anymore,*
*I took a stand*

*I was no longer afraid*
*I had never felt so strong before*
*And I wanted that feeling to stay*
*I had the courage to change my ways*

*The next morning, the sun shined through my window*
*And upon my face*
*I realized in the end I had overcome many struggles*
*And won this tiring race*
*I awoke with a soft smile*
*And what a beautiful way to start my new and brighter days*

Be mindful of the way you treat yourself. Be mindful of the words you use while describing yourself. Be mindful of the tone you set for yourself and others. When you present yourself in a way that exudes self-love, people will match that higher standard in their interactions with you. After complimenting someone else, take a moment to compliment yourself. The more loving words and phrases you use, the more full your inner love tank will be.

In order to truly love who you are today, you need to make peace with your past and forgive the ones who have hurt you. Not necessarily for their gain, but for your own peace of mind. Admit when you have done something wrong and be willing to make things right again. The worst idea to believe is that you are never wrong. How will you ever grow from believing that? Everyone is wrong at some point in their life. It is how we get back up again that matters.

Loving yourself leads to believing in yourself. It's strange how these simple concepts are sometimes the most challenging to achieve. Know what you stand for and be strong in your voice. Believe in yourself and your abilities, even when others doubt you.

People may try to bring you down or tell you you cannot accomplish something that is important to you. They may not understand your reasons or outlook, but here's the good news—they don't have to. Don't seek approval from others if it's something you hold so dear to your heart.

**Value yourself enough to understand your own needs.** Teachers often put the needs of other people before their own. We throw our own needs out the window from the second our students arrive each morning. We go through all the motions of the day without consciously taking breaks for ourselves because of our endless to-do lists. Remember, you can't fully help other people until you yourself are taken care of.

Begin today by taking the next step in developing habits of people who have a strong sense of self-love, so you too can reach the success and happiness you desire in your personal life and your career.

Changing your habits takes a lot of time, patience, and repetition. If it is important enough to you to become a person you love to be, try the two-month self-love habit challenge. That may sound daunting and like a long commitment, but habits take time to become permanent. If you were to do each new habit for only one day, it wouldn't give the lasting change you yearn for.

*Self-Love Habit, Week 1*—focus on reading for a minimum of fifteen minutes a day. I'm sure you can "find the time" by cutting out some of your technology time on social media or watching TV. Read something you enjoy. Something that interests you. Something that inspires you. Go to the self-help section in any bookstore, and you will find countless motivational books to help you lead the life you want to live.

*Self-Love Habit, Week 2*—focus on complimenting others. We live in a world that teaches us to be critical of people and criticize their every move. Instead, mind your own beeswax. Make a point to make someone else feel noticed and special. Be the reason someone else smiles. Let the spotlight shine on others. Continue to read every day during this week.

*Self-Love Habit, Week 3*—focus on embracing change. Moments of change happen all around us. They can be simple or more complex. It is so easy to resist change or try to avoid it because we are comfortable in our ways, but many times there is good that can come from change. We may learn something new about a certain skill or even about ourselves. We simply need to be open to it. Continue to read every day and compliment others.

*Self-Love Habit, Week 4*—focus on forgiving others. Forgiveness is difficult, but can bring about such healing in our hearts. Self-love must be present in order to forgive. Be content with who you are and where you are in life, so you can reap the benefits of such peace and healing. Forgiveness frees you while holding a grudge adds a heavy weight to your shoulders. Continue to read every day, compliment others, and embrace change.

Take a moment to sing Bon Jovi's words with me: "Woah, we're half way there. Woah, livin' on a prayer. Take my hand, we'll make it I swear!" Did I even hear some harmonizing in there? Well done! Now, on to Week 5 of our challenge.

*Self-Love Habit, Week 5*—focus on talking about ideas, not people. The quality of your conversations with other people will immediately be enhanced when the focus is shifted. If you talk about or compare yourself to others, you are only damaging your own self-love. Accept that there is a reason why people think and say what they do. Even if you don't agree with it, you don't have the right to judge them for it until you have walked in their shoes.

Continue to read every day, compliment others, embrace change, and forgive others.

*Self-Love Habit, Week 6*—focus on learning something new. Instead of thinking you know it all, be open to learning about other people's ideas and perspectives. Choose a skill you have always wanted to learn or improve on, and go for it. My great-grandmother lived to be one hundred years old, and she loved to crochet. She would make blankets, tablecloths, hats, and scarves. It was always my goal to learn since she's gone home to Heaven, especially as our first baby was on the way. I know if she were still with us, she would have made an expertly woven blanket for our little munchkin. I was determined to learn. It is a skill I am still practicing during this season of my life. Some people may love learning through travel. Whatever it is that tickles your fancy, take this week to try it. Continue to read every day, compliment others, embrace change, forgive others, and talk about ideas.

*Self-Love Habit, Week 7*—focus on accepting responsibility for your words, actions, and failures. People are so quick to blame others and make excuses as to why they made certain decisions, but this can be damaging. Recognize your thought process while making a decision, understand the situation you were in, and accept the responsibility. For better or for worse. Continue to read every day, compliment others, embrace change, forgive others, talk about ideas, and learn something new.

*Self-Love Habit, Week 8*—focus on feeling grateful for everything. For the good, the bad, and the ugly. Society is full of people who feel entitled. Instead, I encourage you to embrace a sense of gratitude every day and verbalize it. You will gain a whole new perspective on life. A more beautiful one. Continue to read every day, compliment others, embrace change, forgive others, talk about ideas, learn something new, and accept responsibility.

This concludes your two-month self-love habit challenge. However, it doesn't end here. This is only the beginning. Take a moment now to put this challenge into your calendar. Write a quick reminder at the start of each week so you know what your goal and focus should be on for that week.

In order to continue these healthy and positive habits to reach that ultimate self-love, work on setting goals and developing a life plan. You may claim that you are not a planner and that is okay. However, the self-love you hope for may be more attainable by developing a vision for your life and determining the goals that will help get you to where you want to be. To motivate yourself.

People are quick to judge someone who exudes self-love and is confident possibly because they are too scared to step out and openly love themselves. This self-love habit challenge will help you diminish that concern and reach a positive, loving version of yourself.

If you are not into the whole challenge idea, that's all right too. Start by implementing the ideas you feel most comfortable with and slowly introduce the rest into your daily life. Reaching self-love is a different journey for everyone, so be patient with yourself and know that with perseverance you can accomplish anything.

Be your own greatest fan. Love who you are and be grateful to everything that has led you to who you are today. Love yourself unconditionally even when the world tells you not to. It takes courage to love yourself in our world today. Go against what society says you should be like or look like. **Look at yourself and others through a new, more loving filter.** Even if you don't feel beautiful, keep telling yourself that you are, and sooner rather than later you'll start to believe it.

# A Love He's Never Known

When you are able to fully love yourself, then you can spread that love to others. One year, I had a boy in my class, "Ethan," who seemed almost lifeless. He would walk around with his shoulders hunched, and he didn't trust anyone in his life. He had one of the worst home lives I've ever seen.

He would share stories of the past wishing things would go back to when his dad wasn't abusive to his family and an alcoholic. He wished his pet hamsters would be found after being lost in their apartment. I could only imagine what their living condition was like if several hamsters were so easily lost and killed.

Fast-forward to the rest of the school year. I documented every behavior incident in detail and warning sign, and held him through the daily anxiety attacks he experienced. I expressed that Ethan seemed to be a danger to himself. Yet, it felt like I was left to handle it on my own. I would go to work worried about the events that would take place each day. All year I wanted Ethan to undergo a thorough evaluation and get the help he so desperately needed.

After months of this, my voice was finally heard. May 25th was bittersweet. It was a difficult day for Ethan, but little did he know that this was the day his life would change. No, it wouldn't ever be perfect or easy, but it would be one step closer to healing his shattered heart.

Anything would trigger his depression. When Ethan was upset about something small, a flood of horrible memories and traumatic events would take over his mind. Ethan would sulk all day, so instead of forcing curriculum down his throat in these moments, I would set him up with some drawing paper and pillows, making sure he was comfortable and felt safe.

Ethan wrote a very concerning note about how much he hated his family, life, and himself, and how he wanted to kill himself. My stomach immediately sank, bringing back memories of my own. Ethan had written this once before, and I'd been hoping for outside help then, but it was once again brushed aside with no follow-up leaving me to handle it on my own. It's amazing how I was with him the most out of anyone in his life, yet my opinion and desperate concern meant nothing.

People don't realize teachers are voiceless at times and not valued when we know what is best for our cuties. I knew he needed help beyond what our school could provide. Ethan had external counselors come for a safety and risk assessment, but since he didn't have a plan, it looked like once again it was going nowhere.

After dismissal, I met him in the office with the counselors. One counselor asked, "Ethan, is this the teacher you said you could trust and tell your stories to?" He nodded as she explained to me that he said I was the only person in his life that he could trust and talk to. It took months for him to say that aloud, and my heart was so full in that moment. He never seemed to respond to my love and genuine concern because he didn't know how. It was new to him.

While the counselors were meeting and discussing the situation, I played with Ethan and his younger sister, "Tamara." We played Jenga and Guess Who and built towers with blocks while listening to music. Ethan and Tamara were so full of joy. That laughter was the best I've ever heard. We played and played as the time went by. I brought out the side of Ethan I knew was hidden deep inside. It was as if it were the first time anyone had ever sat down to play and talk with them.

The counselors came in to have another discussion with Ethan. He felt scared, but I was able to stay. Listening to him repeat the stories he had recited to me all year long was when I kept thinking to myself, "How could they not get him help?"

Ethan was so brave and honest, which helped him get the help he needed ... finally. The one counselor explained to him how his life was like a plate full of cookies and each cookie was a different story from his broken life. His plate was so high and he was so full that he couldn't carry the plate anymore.

She asked him, "How would you feel if I say you need to go to the hospital?" Ethan explained that his older sister went there once because she "had hard times and needed help handling it."

As soon as I assured him he would be safe there and cared for, he collapsed into my arms crying and said, "Yes, I'm ready. How long can I stay?" There was not a dry eye in the room. That simple answer changed the course of his life. They left the room, and I stayed with him.

Ethan started to shake, so I told him to ask any questions he had and talk out any worries he had. He asked, "How long will I be there? How long can I stay? What if I feel scared at night? Am I going to come back? Is it far?"

Ethan was happy to hear about the nurse call button on the side of the bed. I assured him he could hold onto his favorite stuffed animals that were already luckily in his backpack. As I held him closely like a mother should, I kept repeating, "You are going to feel so safe at the hospital. They are going to take such good care of you and help you learn how to handle your feelings."

The counselors told his mom about the situation and that she needed to take him to the hospital. She complained about the inconvenience and made every excuse not to go. They warned her that the hospital already knew he was on his way, so if she didn't bring him, they would contact her. As the counselor sent them on their way, all of us looked at each other, admitting that she wasn't going to take him.

The one counselor admitted, "What was I thinking letting them go?"

I quickly asked, "Can I please go get them?"

As the yes came out of her mouth I was already out the door. I told our principal to come with me just in case the mom caused a scene. I ran out of the school looking frantically in every direction. Where did they go? How did they get so far? As I spotted them down the road, I ran to them while calling for Ethan. I've never run that fast in my life.

I motioned for them to come back, and Ethan ran to me leaving his mom and Tamara behind. He was shaking by the time he got to me, startled by the whole scene. I explained to him that we were going to get a police officer to take him, so we would know that he reached the hospital since his mom had been complaining of having to pay for a taxi. He admitted that he was scared to be with her as he begged, "Don't leave me with her! Please don't!" I assured him I wouldn't leave his side until the car came, and we returned to school.

He chose to stay with me in a separate room from his mother and sister. When three police cars showed up, Ethan hid under the table. He was used to cops coming to his house looking for his dad, so he was fearful of them. He started worrying, if his mom went to jail, then who would he live with? When they came into the office, I asked if I could introduce Ethan to them.

The police officer that came in was an angel sent from above. He said, "What's up, dude? I'm Frank," motioning for a high five. I could have cried in that moment knowing he would win the trust of Ethan.

I explained to Ethan that Frank would bring him to the hospital and make sure he was safe there.

Ethan looked at me and asked, "Are you sure he's a good guy?"

I answered, "Of course he is! I wouldn't let him take you if he was anything but amazing!"

I walked with him to the police car. Frank told Ethan that he would open the window between the seats, so he could talk to Ethan during the drive.

As we walked out of the school, his mom and sister followed behind us. Ethan was mumbling to me, "Please don't let her go in my car."

A different police officer suggested, "Why don't we have his mom and sister go in my car, and Frank can take Ethan?"

Ethan heard this and mumbled to me, "Yes, please. That's perfect."

Without saying goodbye to his mother, Ethan stepped into the police car. I helped him in with his stuffed animal, Foxy, and Frank helped buckle his seat. I asked him if he had any other questions before he went, and he nodded no. I told him how brave he was and how safe he would feel at the hospital.

As I closed the door, I felt the strongest love for him and knew that this was the most love he'd ever felt in his life. My close colleague told me, "He did say goodbye to his "mom," he said goodbye to you. You're the closest thing he has to a mother." With that realization and after holding it all in, I let go and cried for this little boy.

It was now well past dinnertime. We sat still in the heaviness of the situation. The counselor told me that never in all her years of doing this did a teacher stay with her during the entire safety and risk assessment. I knew it could've been a different result if I had left. I was his number one advocate. I needed to be his champion. He needed me now more than ever before.

The next two days I checked in with the hospital to make sure he was still there and was told he didn't have visitors. Immediately, I put together a backpack full of cards from our class, activities, coloring paper, crayons, and books about hamsters to keep him busy. As I entered the door to his hospital room, I saw his artwork hanging up around the room on foam food trays. He was so excited to have a visitor and told his nurse all about our class while I was there.

I made sure he had enough water and crackers and even asked the nurse for a new gown since his was all ripped. Things a mother would do. I told him the next time I would see him would be when he returns to school and our class couldn't wait to have him back. After spending a week in the hospital waiting on approval from his parents, he was sent to a two-week psych placement to further address his depression.

Once again, I've learned that the children are the teachers too. I learned to be patient with Ethan, continue to give love even when he seemed resistant, never give up on a child, uncover the root of his negative behaviors, stay true to what I believed in, and love unconditionally.

**The greatest gift you can give someone is the gift of your love.**

Any time I would try to help him turn a negative thought positive and find the good in a difficult situation or believe in himself, Ethan wanted nothing to do with it. He would be unresponsive and hide in the classroom to avoid any interactions with others. He would negate any comment I made about being there for him or caring for him.

Ethan was an unbelievable artist, something I encouraged throughout the school year to help him express himself, but he would draw the most dark and twisted pictures. One in particular will remain in my mind forever. He drew himself curled up on the floor against a closed door with his head leaning on his knees. He wrote the word "worry" across his face with tears streaming down from his eyes. These drawings broke my heart but didn't stop my efforts. I continued to love him every step of the way. I would use up every ounce of my energy to show love and compassion to this little boy.

When you think you are not getting through to a student or they are not listening to what you say, they are. When you think they are not receptive to what you are giving them, they are. They may not show it in that moment, but they hear you. They see the effort you are putting in. Give them time to process it in their own way.

Six months later, I received the following letter:

Hi Mrs. Gano,

I really miss you. I hope you have a great time with your students. I'll always let you be in my heart. I don't know what to say, but I wish I was your son. I changed a lot including my art. I will send you some art. Also, my depression is getting lower and you helped me a lot and made me change every day. You gave me the light to be free and loved. I hope you finished your house. Please send me back a letter.

Love,
Ethan

As you could imagine, tears were instantly streaming down my face upon reading this letter. I was overwhelmed with the realization I waited so long for him to have: Ethan let love in. All of my effort, tears, and sleepless nights were worth it. I wrote back to him right away thrilled that he was reaching out like I had never seen before.

He responded with this letter and more artwork. In one of the new pictures, he drew himself curled up on the floor with the word "empty" across his face and tears streaming down from his eyes. Then, there was an arrow pointing to a drawing of me holding him and saying, "I will always love you." Both of us have smiles on our faces. His art really did change. It was brighter.

> Hi Mrs. Gano,
>
> I really miss you sooooooooooooooooooooooooooo muuuuuuuuuuuuuuuuch. I love you and miss you. I cried (almost) when you gave me the letter. It's like when I'm broken, I found a connection. For example, I'm a heart that is broken from damage and people, but I found the right direction and you were the one who helped me. Thank you.
>
> Love,
> Ethan

After realizing that love is louder than the negativity in this world, I wrote this poem when I was in college. I was reminded of this poem in my experiences with Ethan. Love has the power to help us face any obstacle and look beyond the darkest clouds knowing we are not alone.

## Love Is Louder

*Love is louder than this place called fear*
*Love is louder than pain, violence, and tears*
*Love is louder than words that bring you down*
*Know that you are never alone*
*as each day comes around*

*I know you're scared right now*
*But it's going to be alright*
*Just lean on me*
*And I'll help you get through this fight*

*Remember you are strong enough*
*to let go of the ones who hurt you*
*And try to break you down*
*When you look in the mirror,*
*do you see your incredible value?*
*Gather your strength from within*
*to stand up for what you know is right*
*Hold on to the ones you love*
*when you know it is true*
*And know that God is always looking down*
*from above protecting you*

*Love brings a smile to your face*
*And adds a sparkle to your eyes*
*It gives you hope*
*And your heart has wings to fly*

*Hold your head up high and be brave*
*Wipe those tears from your eyes*

*Please don't be afraid*
*I am here to remind you*
*That love will protect you from harm*

*Love is louder*
*Everyone deserves to feel it*
*Embrace the love around you and truly believe*
*You can feel love from miles away*
*And it will help get you through each and every day*

If you use anything from this chapter, please let it be this: look in the mirror and see the beauty and wonder that you are. Be proud of the long battle you overcame in loving yourself. If you haven't quite made it there yet, take the first step in doing so. Self-love is the foundation to living a fulfilled and more positive life at work, at home, everywhere.

When your love tank is full, you can make a difference in other people's lives. **Work on being in love with the person in the mirror who has been through so much but is still standing tall.** That is true beauty. Choose yourself over and over again. Build your self-esteem one baby step at a time. Soon you will look back and see how far you have come.

## *Self-Reflect*

- Where are you in your journey to finding self-love?
- How often do you build yourself up with kind words and positive thoughts?
- How you treat yourself is how others will treat you. What tone do you set?
- How can you encourage others to master their own self-love?

## *Take Action*

- Find acceptance for the past, peace for the present, and hope for the future.
- Be self-aware by knowing your strengths and weaknesses and understanding what your needs are.
- Be mindful of the words you use while describing yourself.
- Take the self-love habit challenge.
- Forgive the people who have hurt you.
- Set goals and develop a life plan in order to continue these positive habits to reach self-love.
- Be patient with yourself and celebrate small successes along the way.

# 10. Your Need to Breathe

"That's not fair!" How many times a day do your students utter these words? You would be so rich that you could quit your job completely if you got paid every time you heard it being yelled across your exquisitely planned-out classroom. I'm about to tell you something that might not seem *fair*, but it's all part of the survival mode teachers find themselves in.

**You must make time to rest, relax, and repeat.** Notice that I didn't say *find* the time to. If I did, you could easily go about your day saying, "Oh well, there was no time" or "I couldn't find the time to do it." You're absolutely right. Most days you feel like you're back on that treadmill that's going way too fast while dodging all the things being thrown your way.

Yes, it is fair! *You* matter! If you're not mentally relaxed, the whole school day will be a hot mess. By taking care of yourself in those small moments, you're benefiting your students, colleagues, lunch aides, custodians, and anyone you come in contact with each day. Positivity is contagious.

I make a point in my classroom to make my own need to breathe a teaching point for my students. When I feel like I need a moment, I verbalize that so my students can see a healthy way of dealing with stress. I say something like, "I'm feeling like I need a moment to calm down and breathe," and invite them to join me if they are experiencing similar feelings. I then model taking a deep breath and repeating it three times. Then I verbalize how much that helped me, gave me that little boost I was longing for to continue on in my day.

I also play relaxing music in my classroom. I have it playing softly in the background, which sets a calm tone. The munchkins love this! When they go off and do work on their own, they're always asking if they can listen to calming music while they work. I love when they ask this because I know I am instilling a love of relaxing music in their cute little hearts that will last beyond the school year. They leave my classroom knowing they can use this coping technique when feeling overwhelmed at home or in future situations.

Teachers rarely think about their own needs throughout the school day. We rarely put ourselves first because our main priority is the safety and education of our students. I'm sure you can easily relate to this. You say goodbye to your own needs from the moment you arrive. Even the most basic needs like drinking enough water or escaping for less than a minute to use the bathroom while being questioned by your students on where you are going while your work friend covers your class.

A wise colleague once told me, "You can't pour from an empty glass." That is so very true. In order to stay sane and be able to continue your day successfully, it is imperative to take those short moments to breathe. Self-care makes all the difference! Rest your mind and body by practicing basic breathing techniques. Find ways to relax that help you restore your energy and focus.

One way you can do this is making time to be in a quiet setting, maybe while the children are at their special or lunch. I've done this in the past by setting aside one day a week that I eat lunch in my classroom. It's a quiet and peace I long for and look forward to. During this time, reflect on your day noting the good and bad parts, so you can learn from them. Reconnect with yourself and your needs.

Like many teachers do, I find it more work to be absent than actually in school. Plans for substitute teachers can take hours of your precious time. I've always pondered how teachers use all of their personal days because they know they'll lose them the following year in most cases. I shy away from that idea. Except one day this year.

I was helping Brandon at an all-day live screen printing work event at a youth football tournament for his business, Twisted Ink Screen Printing and Embroidery, on the weekend. I knew my pregnant self would struggle getting through a full week of school after this action-packed weekend.

I anticipated this as a potential issue, so I put in my request for a personal day for the following Tuesday. We are denied personal days often in this district especially on Mondays and Fridays ... and almost any day that ends in a y for that matter. They also have a rule that no more than five teachers can be out in the entire district, so I didn't bank on it to work out but I certainly hoped it would. That's beside the point.

I booked my first prenatal massage for that day and planned to have a day of relaxation. I thought to myself, *Who am I? Who cares! I'm loving this!* As I lay on the massage table ready to drift off into pure bliss and escape any worries on my mind, I was thinking of you. Yes, you!

How I wish every teacher would treat themselves to a personal day and do something for themselves for once. It was self-care at its finest. Sometimes we need to acknowledge our own needs and accept that we would be better off taking a day than pushing through a day feeling overwhelmed and exhausted. In that moment, I understood the fabulous effects of self-care.

## Movin' and Groovin'

Sometimes it feels so satisfying to just punch something. In boxing, of course! During my post-college years living back at home, I found myself experiencing some built-up baggage from the past. I wasn't interested in frequent exercise because I hadn't found something I enjoyed doing yet.

I have always loved movies about boxing and the main character's transformation would inspire me. How they used their struggles to fuel the fire within and never give up. One day I decided to try it myself. I went to a weekly class at a local Title Boxing and learned all of the basic moves for boxing and kick-boxing.

Man, did it feel amazing! I felt brave, tough, powerful, but mostly proud that I tried something new. I found a healthy outlet to release that extra energy. Getting my heart rate up and adrenaline flowing was healing in a new, intriguing way.

My extent of exercise prior to this was, well, nonexistent, so I was thrilled to have sparked a new interest. I even treated myself to my own punching bag at home. Now, I save myself some money by boxing in the comfort of my home. Whatever your outlet is, find it and embrace it because simply put ... you need it and you deserve it.

## Breathing In and Out

A popular buzzword used lately in education is mindfulness and, boy, am I glad it is! I have learned the power of mindfulness and brought it into my daily classroom routine. What a difference it has made. Teaching children (and yourself!) about mindfulness models healthy habits and coping strategies for them to use throughout their lives.

I went to a professional development on mindfulness and yoga in the classroom in my district. It was like spending an hour in paradise! The tone you set, the calmness in your voice can create the most effective learning/teaching space for your students and yourself.

As I've mentioned earlier, breathing is often taken for granted. We know our bodies will do it on their own without much thought involved. However, when you are intentional with the way you breathe, you have some serious power!

You can get yourself all hyped up for a big event or dance party by breathing in and out quickly. Or you can calm your mind and body by breathing in and out slowly. This type of breathing takes practice. Hence, mindfulness and yoga! The newfound loves of my life. Please don't tell my husband what he's competing against.

Picture your mind filled with glitter because life is simply better with glitter. When you are calm, the glitter is settled at the bottom of your head. If you shake it up and feel angry or stressed out, the glitter will swirl around like a tornado gone wild.

It is our responsibility to calm our minds and help the glitter settle to the bottom again. You can do this by breathing with intention. When you model healthy breathing techniques, it will enhance your own self-care and teach your students to do the same.

Breathing beads will become your new best friend. I learned about this practice at a Mindfulness and Yoga PD in my school and saw the positive impact it had on my own classroom. Now, it's your turn to share it with *your* world. Breathing beads are made using a half of a pipe cleaner and six beads. Be sure to roll the ends of the pipe cleaner so the beads don't fall off. Push the beads to the left. Each bead represents a breath in or out.

As you move the first bead slowly to the right, take a deep breath in. Then move the second bead slowly and breathe out. Move the third bead while taking a deep, slow breath in. Then move the fourth bead and breathe out. Move the fifth bead while taking a deep breath in. Then move the sixth bead and breathe out.

Instantly, that glitter will have settled in your radiant mind, and a calmness will wash over you like a warm, fuzzy blanket on a cold day. **The comfort and peace this brings has the power to change the course of your mindset and your day.**

I made breathing beads with my students, and they loved them so much that they asked to make more, so they could bring their second set home. They started throwing their poor family members under the bus by saying, "My dad could really use this!" And, "I want to show my brother. He gets so mad when he does his homework." One girl even said, "I want to show this to my friend because sometimes we get into arguments." Spread the word, my little ducklings! The world needs more of this.

My students know they can use the breathing beads in their desks whenever they feel they need a moment to calm themselves. It brings me great joy to see them use it without me prompting them. One time they were taking a test and a few of my students took their breathing beads out, took those healthy breaths in and out, then continued on their test. One girl even told me that she had a hard time falling asleep at night because it was so noisy in her neighborhood, but she now used her breathing beads every night.

Some other favorite breathing techniques that are easy to use in the classroom are roller coaster breathing, rainbow breathing, and the firework. For roller coaster breathing, put your hand in front of you and spread out your fingers. Trace the outside of your fingers with your other pointer finger. Take a deep, slow breath in as you trace *up* each finger and take a slow breath out as you trace *down* each finger.

For rainbow breathing, stand up tall. Breathe in as you extend your arms long and up, bringing your hands together above your head. Then breathe out as you bring your arms back down to your side making a rainbow shape.

For firework breathing, start curled up crouching on the floor. Take a deep, slow breath while hugging your knees in a ball. Then breathe out while springing your body up and spreading your arms and legs out like a big X. Of course, making a firework sound can add a more dramatic effect.

These breathing techniques will work for you in your own life and for your students in your classroom. Encourage this! It will surely improve the zoo-like behavior you may be experiencing in your wonderfully decorated classroom. I've put my trust in the power of breathing and mindfulness. I hope you do too.

Years ago, my neighbor asked me to go to a free yoga class one Saturday morning. I had always wanted to try yoga, but never brought myself to actually go. I wasn't sure if I would be "good at it." Or at least that's the excuse I was using for a while. Absolutely life-changing.

Having an hour in a quiet, peaceful space focusing solely on resting my body and mind was Heaven on Earth. Stretching every part of my body, most that had never been given attention before all while focusing on my breathing was simply magical.

The moment I experienced my first Savasana I was mesmerized. Savasana is the Sanskrit name of the final pose of most yoga classes. It's also called "lying down" pose because you lie in a neutral position on your back with your arms and legs long and resting loosely on the floor. That's the whole pose. Simple yet powerful.

Savasana is all about relaxing your whole body and calming your mind. All of your everyday worries seem to escape your mind as you lie there in pure relaxation and bliss. I learned a new mathematical equation that day:

**Savasana + Lavender essential oil = Paradise**

On my way out of the yoga class, I bought a ten-class card and began going every week. Looking forward to that blissful feeling every Thursday was what helped me handle anything that week threw at me. Yoga has a powerful way of putting your mind at ease and delving into the most rewarding self-care session.

I incorporate yoga, breathing, and simple meditation into my classroom, which has benefited me and my students. These healthy practices awaken you and your students' minds and allow for even more learning.

## Affirmations

Learning the power of affirmations has greatly impacted my life, and it can do the same for yours. In recent years, I've learned the importance of reciting affirmations aloud and seen the positive shift it can create. I have a list of *I am* and *I will* statements that I recite every morning to start my day on a positive note. The key is to read them aloud and with passion.

In the beginning, you might not believe every word completely, but that's just your mind defaulting to the limiting self-beliefs you have adopted over the years. Do your best to ignore these. The more you read your affirmations, the more you believe in them and in yourself. Remember to be patient. Change won't come right away.

Affirmations can be used in your classroom as well. My students read in unison a list of whole class affirmations before we start our day. That idea stemmed from realizing the pain and hardships many of my students bring to school each day. If I could teach them how to be positive even on a difficult day and *look beyond the clouds*, then I can sleep well knowing they will carry that lesson throughout their life.

You can teach affirmations and goal setting using an *I am, I will* activity. Brainstorm ideas as a class, then have students write their own statements. Hang them up where they will see theirs each day, whether it be on their desk or in their cubby or locker. **The more you *say it*, the more you'll *believe it* and the more you'll *live it*.**

Remember to keep your statements specific and attainable. If you say, "I am a millionaire" and there is only one-hundred dollars in your bank account, then your brain will recognize that and automatically defeat the purpose of the activity.

The following examples will help get you started. They can be used as either whole class affirmations or individual affirmations depending on what each child wants to focus on. I would suggest selecting five or six affirmations for your whole class list to keep it concise. Each child's individual list can include however many they see fit.

## *I am ...*

*I am loved, safe, and cared for.*
*I am fortunate to have supportive people in my life.*
*I am loving and kind.*
*I am able to think and speak positively.*
*I am intelligent.*
*I am focused on the good in every situation.*

*I am proud of my accomplishments.*

*I am a hard worker.*

*I am capable of doing anything I set my mind to.*

*I am confident in the person I am.*

*I am brave to accept challenges.*

*I am a good friend to others.*

*I am healthy and take care of my body and mind.*

## I will ...

*I will* look beyond the clouds *when faced with a challenge or difficult day.*

*I will study my multiplication facts, so I do well on my test.*

*I will listen and pay attention in class, so I can learn.*

*I will complete my homework four times this week.*

*I will be respectful to myself and others.*

*I will take responsibility for my words and actions.*

Go to www.lookbeyondtheclouds.com to download my personal affirmations and try them for yourself.

## Decluttering Your Life

For all of you organization lovers with undiagnosed OCD, this one's for you. I love organizing. You may roll your eyes at me or you may praise me for my love of organized bins and rainbow-ordered everything. This is where that self-love piece comes in. I've accepted (and love) that I'm a strange human who gets excited to organize just about anything.

The satisfaction and peace of mind that come from removing clutter leaves me on cloud nine for a while. So carry on as you wish, but I hope you join me up on cloud nine—as well as *beyond the clouds!*—every so often. We can enjoy the *breathtaking view* together.

My advice to you: declutter your life! I'm not only saying this because I vividly remember the days of nesting and preparing for our baby to be born. Preggo or not, decluttering and organizing will leave you feeling lighter and happier. Yes, this takes time, but it is worth every second of it! You are more likely to be productive and feel relaxed when your workspace—your desk, whiteboard, classroom walls—is clutter-free.

This also goes for your mind, too. If your mind is full of daily concerns, worries, and stressors, you are unable to function at your full potential. Take five minutes each morning to acknowledge the worries that consume your mind, write them down, and prioritize steps of how you can tackle them in the coming few days.

I am a proud to-do list queen. Lists help me keep track of everything that is on my mind (worries, things I need to get done, ideas), then move on without the added worry of forgetting what I needed to remember. Yes, this worry is a common occurrence in my brain if a list isn't made. It's about being self-aware and knowing your strengths and weaknesses, right?

You will find an ongoing to-do list on my classroom desk at all times. As ideas or reminders pop into my head mid-lesson, I take a second to jot it down. At the end of the day, I prioritize the items that *must* be done today and then set goals for what I would like to complete by the following day, week, and so on.

I'm that person who completes my work well in advance of when it's actually due. Then I hear, "Ugh, I hate you. How are you done with that already? I haven't even started it!" Well, it's simple, people! *You* are in control. Organize yourself and set goals for each day to get it done ahead of time. Manage your time well.

Time management is such a cleansing skill. It leads to the extraordinary effects of decluttering your life. It's something we talk to our students about, so we already know it's a habit we should be practicing—not just preaching—as well!

## Creative Juices Flowing

I love coloring books. Yes, I am a full-grown adult. I can't help but wonder who was the Debbie Downer who made the unspoken rule that coloring and being creative is for kids only? I'm not buying it! Never have, never will. Children are full of imagination and creativity while many adults lose that interest with age. I, on the other hand, didn't seem to fall into that category. I've used coloring, solving puzzles, and crafting to explore my creative side and as my go-to forms of relaxation.

When you focus carefully on something like coloring a picture or completing a puzzle, it gives you a break from everyday worries, which gives your mind the much-needed rest it requires. It really helped my "cool" status when adult coloring books became a real thing in society. I guess I could take credit for being such a trendsetter!

It is my hope that you figure out a way to express yourself creatively, whether it be with music, acting, crocheting, painting, scrapbooking, designing, decorating, baking, and so on. The opportunities are out there. Take a moment to see which one fits your strengths and enjoy the time doing something you love. To return to my wise colleague's words, "You can't pour from an empty glass."

# Big Dreams

We, as teachers, encourage our students to follow their dreams and reach for the stars, but somehow forget to follow our own advice. Part of self-care is *making* the time to follow a dream you keep putting off. Don't keep saying things like, "I wish I could (fill in awesome goal here)." Just. Do. It.

I know a million excuses are filling your lovely mind right now, but do your best to silence them. Start by taking one step toward reaching that dream. You have too many gifts and talents to share with the world. You spend every day for other people. Now, it's *your* time.

One summer, I set the goal of filing for a patent with the United States Patent and Trademark Office. I believed in my idea so much that I knew I needed to share it with the world. Thus, the terrifying prospect of navigating the patent application process.

Brandon bought me *Patents, Copyrights, and Trademarks for Dummies.* **I don't even know how to repay him for the number of times he has supported my crazy ideas with more love and encouragement than I could imagine.** I have the best number one fan ever.

Anywho, I read this book from front to back and followed every step in the process. I went from "dummy" to quite knowledgeable. I spent all summer researching, reviewing an extensive patent search, proving how my invention was different than the fifty other inventions that had similar keywords listed, filling out forms, getting professional drawings with insane detail, and writing the lengthy specification. I endured this tedious three-year process—yes, three years—which, in the end, became way too expensive to complete for a "maybe."

For anyone wondering, "Any regrets about that, Michelle?" you should already know: no way.

Summer seems to be the time when I dream big. Another summer I began my journey of writing this book you hold in your hand. I loved my routine of starting each day with stretching and yoga, boxing, then ten minutes on our elliptical. Then I'd sit down and write my heart out. It was such a healing and creative process.

September came and writing was put on hold. I was pregnant at this point and sleeping every chance I could get to ease the nausea. Also, wishing I could spend my days writing to finish what I had started that summer. I started making excuses and catching myself saying things like, "Maybe it's not meant to happen right now." Or "I need to focus on resting and not push myself too much."

October hit me like a ton of bricks. Enough was enough! I'm not one for making excuses! I couldn't keep putting this dream off. Instead, I used my pregnancy as motivation. If I waited until after our baby boy was born, then who knows when it would be done, if ever.

I had just overcome the morning sickness, or in my case, all-day nausea, of my first trimester, so nothing would stop me now. I felt like a super human, and I wasn't willing to slow down and plan a pity party for myself. Woman up and quit making excuses. **There are no valid excuses when it comes to accomplishing your dreams.**

On October 11, I mentioned it to my number one fan when we were eating dinner and reflecting on our day. I had been listening to a podcast for Chandler Bolt's Self-Publishing School (SPS) every morning on my way to work, so I wondered if it was something I could pursue to help me get back on track with completing and publishing my book.

When Brandon and I looked it up, we discovered a free webinar would be taking place starting fifteen minutes from then. We looked at each other in awe and scrambled to set things up in time for the webinar.

I was willing to do the dirty work and take over the world! ... Or at least my own world and mindset. The fire reignited in my heart but to an extreme. I knew nothing, not even an excuse, could stop me this time. I was unstoppable.

On October 12, I had a breakthrough session with one of Self-Publishing School's finest, Brett, to discuss my hopes in becoming an author and a motivational speaker for teachers and children, what I've written so far, and to see if I would be a good fit for the program.

I had the most inspiring, motivational conversation with Brett. He said I was like a racehorse ready to dart out of its stall. I just needed direction with the process of editing, formatting, launching, publishing, and so on to make it happen. He couldn't have described it any better!

By the end of the phone call I registered, paying more than I knew we could afford. When checking with Brandon with my best puppy dog eyes ever to make sure we could swing the cost, he urged me, "Do it. I believe in what you are about to become. Let me worry about the money part. All it means is I'll have to work extra to make it happen. Power team, right?" I will never forget the belief in his eyes in that moment.

Following the SPS program with step-by-step videos would ensure that this dream would become a reality sooner than we had originally hoped. Just in time to welcome our baby boy into the world in April.

I had my first video call with my coach, Lise, on October 24. She set high expectations and assured me that continuing my writing schedule of writing from five o'clock to six o'clock each morning would be enough to compile a rough draft and start the self-editing phase.

I wrote like I had never written before. I was a crazy lady motivated more than ever with two babies in progress ... my human one and now, my book baby. I knew I'd made the right choice signing up with SPS for this adventure. In taking part in some self-care, I knew the echo of my message would benefit so many incredible teachers and students.

From having this dream to taking that first step toward reaching it, I sent off my book baby to the editor by December 12. It's amazing to see how taking one baby step can actually be a giant leap toward achieving your greatest goals.

I share my experience with the patent process and writing this book because I want you to know that *it is possible*. Whatever dream you've been putting off can be achieved if you take that first step. **Self-care is about living your life with purpose and acknowledging your own needs.**

You'll be surprised at how helping yourself allows you to be more available to help those around you. A happier, more fulfilled you will emerge. Set an example for your own children and for the students in your class. Model these healthy habits for the little munchkins who look up to you so much. Set goals and care enough about yourself to see them through. You deserve it.

And remember, it *is* fair.

## Self-Reflect

- How do you like to exercise and get your body moving?
- In what ways do you like to express yourself creatively?
- What breathing techniques will you use to calm the glitter in your brain?
- What morning routine or practice gets you ready to start your day on a positive note?
- Reflect on how engaging in each of these practices enhances your physical, emotional, and spiritual sides.

# Take Action

- Make breathing beads for yourself and with your students—and then use them regularly.

- Practice the various breathing techniques and choose your favorites.

- Attend a yoga class and experience Savasana.

- Treat yourself to lavender essential oil. My favorite brand is Aura Cacia. They even have bath powder and shower tablets if you want to full out spoil yourself!

- Make a list of affirmations for yourself and for your class.

- Make a list of *I am* and *I will* statements. Read them aloud every morning. Include statements you might not necessarily believe yet. After time and repetition, you will start to feel more confident and believe in each one.

- Declutter your life. Take five minutes each morning to write down the worries that consume your mind. Prioritize steps of how you will shorten your list.

- Address your own needs by regularly engaging in your favorite self-care practices.

# 11. *In the Sunshine*

I had the pleasure of speaking with "Barbara" a seasoned school counselor about my book in progress. Immediately, Barbara shared examples from her own career that reinforce our mission: when teachers support their fellow teachers to see the positive, everyone moves from dark clouds to the sunshine. The school becomes a happier, more invigorated community for all (okay ... for most) its members. Let's look at two of Barbara's experiences.

## A Hefty Lift

The first story Barbara recalled was when a colleague of hers, Sarah, was reassigned to a new grade level after being comfortable and capable in the same grade for almost ten years. Sarah received little explanation as to why she was moved. Feeling discouraged by the change placed upon her by administration, Sarah couldn't help but question, "Is it me? Am I not doing a good job? Should I even be teaching anymore?"

Barbara raved about how creative this teacher was and how heartbreaking it was to hear her questioning her worth as a teacher. Sarah enjoyed teaching with a hands-on approach always including a kinesthetic aspect to her lessons. She had the ability to reach more students' needs with this type of teaching. It was evident Sarah's students benefited greatly from her well-considered, creative lessons.

When Sarah looked to Barbara and her colleagues for support and encouragement, they reminded her of this strength, which in turn helped ease her worries about not being good enough. A smooth transition was now possible for her. Again, this teacher-on-teacher reassurance offers the lift and the light that each of us needs at different times in our days, weeks, and careers. As Sarah's colleagues did for her, when we support one another, the resulting effect is a hefty forward and upward lift beyond those dismal clouds.

## Dragging Red vs. Elevating Blue

Barbara's second story took place earlier in her career when she worked alongside a fellow school counselor, Janet. Janet was your typical negative red balloon teacher, always counting down the seconds to her retirement. Riding it out until she could finally be done and all the while trying to drag everyone else down to her unhappy level. But it wasn't only Janet's incessant complaining that Barbara had to endure. Additionally, Janet would pour her own responsibilities onto Barbara's plate since Barbara was newer to the school.

Barbara's mentor, Anna, a math teacher, assured her that not all the teachers were negative like Janet. Anna was a positive blue balloon teacher who went out of her way to take people under her wing and help them be successful. She didn't want the cranky teachers to corrupt anyone else. Anna didn't need to verbalize this because her positivity was clear by the example she led.

As Anna didn't want Barbara to be taken advantage of, she stood up for Barbara and told her that Janet's assigned tasks weren't Barbara's responsibility and that it was too much for Barbara to attempt to take on both her own workload plus Janet's demands. Anna gave Barbara that much needed teacher-on-teacher support at a critical time in Barbara's early career.

Admittedly, her Janet dealings also taught Barbara that even the most optimistic of teachers will encounter red balloon teachers and the weight of their negativity does have some influence. Red balloons seek to find one another and make their voices heard. Misery loves company.

However, Barbara's experience showed that the positive and hopeful can and will prevail: there are positive, helpful teachers out there who are ready to light others' worlds. We need to find other diamonds in the rough (teachers like you!) and inspire our colleagues to emulate that goodness and adapt the same positive mindset by transforming their daily habits. Yes, we return to the chain reaction of changed reactions!

Barbara's stories are relatable and intertwined with a common theme, our theme: teacher-on-teacher support can make all the difference in your mindset as you navigate the daily experiences in the stress-filled world of teaching. We all have that teacher friend that we can turn to when our view is clouded and we need help reaching the sunshine beyond. Let's join together making every effort to offer lift and light!

## Basking in the Glow

Live in the sunshine. This is a choice we all have. Every human being in this splendid world experiences darkness at some point throughout their lifetime, some more often than others. It is how we overcome this darkness that creates the foundation of our future.

If Ethan can find the light, then anyone can. Ethan is no longer in my school since he moved onto the next grade, but I was recently graced with a surprise visit from him shortly after receiving the heartwarming letters. During dismissal, a colleague popped into my room and squealed, "Ethan is outside!"

I quickly jumped from my desk and ran out to see him before his bus left. He ran to me and gave me the biggest hug while tears fell from his eyes. He shared, "I just told them how I wish you were here, so I could see you and then out you came!" I thanked him for his letters and commended his new artwork. Ethan gushed about how much he missed being in my class and how he's really trying to be happy.

In that moment I experienced flashbacks to those sleepless nights where I felt like I was fighting an interminable battle. Just as quickly, my anxiety was eased when I heard the eloquent lyrics of Andrea Day's song "Rise Up" play in my mind, as it had each time I would hold Ethan through his anxiety attacks: "I'll rise up. In spite of the ache. I'll rise up and I'll do it a thousand times again. For you."

I didn't want this moment to end. I know Ethan's road will never be easy, but I am hopeful that he will continue to overcome the mountains he'll face. Similarly I am hopeful that by sharing Ethan's story with you, you are inspired to spread the love, sunshine, and hope both to your colleagues and your students, even the ones who seem most clouded in pain and difficulty. Let me state it a second time: if Ethan can find the light, then anyone—and everyone—can, especially when given the much-appreciated love and support.

If you choose to live in the darkness and surround yourself with negativity, you will miss out on all the opportunities this world has to offer. If you choose to live in the sunshine and surround yourself with positivity, you will live the fulfilled life you've always dreamed of—at work, at home, everywhere. You will develop a stronger sense of who you are, rather than who society wants you to be.

**As teachers, we are selfless miracle workers. We put the needs of others before our own. Each day. Each week. Each month. Each year. It's only a matter of time before we feel completely worn out.**

The moment we think of our own needs first, we feel selfish and ashamed and default to our usual thinking of putting our own self-care last. What I have learned from this roller coaster of ups and downs called Life is that, in fact, true happiness and peace come when we take time for ourselves to heal and work toward the positive, fulfilling life we've always hoped for but never quite reached.

Together, we can make a difference. We can be the change. We can bring people out of the darkness and into the brightest, most glorious light. My hope is that you apply these concepts to your teaching experiences as well as your personal life starting today. Enlist a friend or group of colleagues to join this movement with you. We can't do this alone.

Challenge yourself to *look beyond the clouds* and live in the sunshine, finding the good in every situation. Having the right mindset will help you face obstacles, overcome the darkness, and reach a life more magnificent than you could have ever imagined for yourself. I'm living proof of this. Grateful doesn't even begin to express how I feel to have the opportunity to share my mindset and life with you. To empower you. To help you know you are not alone.

We are on this lifelong journey of learning and growing each day. I consider myself one of the few lucky ones in this complex world who live out the life they have always dreamed of. Will you join me? You are already on your way by reading this book. Step one, check! Prepare yourself to continue to dig deep, face your fears head-on, self-reflect, and take action, all the while making time to nurture and care for yourself.

If you have had a little voice in your head telling you to improve your situation at home or at school, please remember that life and time are two of the most precious gifts you will be given. Don't waste them. This is not a dress rehearsal, people! It's opening night at the sold-out show.

Don't be the person who looks back on the years thinking of all the things they wish they'd done. Be the person who looks back with a smile on their face and a tear in their eye, saying, "Wow, look what I have accomplished."

Many times in life we are so concerned with pleasing other people and being what they want us to be. From this moment on, I want you to start making choices that please *you* and guide *you* to a life you want to live. What gets you out of bed in the morning? Go after it with all your heart.

## Inspiration Station

Addressing your own needs and making yourself feel fulfilled positively impacts the people around you and allows you to better serve them—your students, colleagues, family, friends, community, and the world as a whole. By engaging in self-love and self-care, you can create a life you don't need a vacation from.

My hope is for you to make a promise to yourself that you will start taking small steps toward this. Be prepared to heal the wounds of your own past. Find out what your passion is and determine what the first step is in making it a reality in your classroom and personal life. **If your dreams don't scare you a little bit, they aren't big enough.** You have the ability to reach the peace and happiness you've always longed for. Don't let anything "get in the way" of your happiness this time!

When you work toward your greatest, most fulfilled self, you inspire others to do the same. If you have lost the spark and forgotten why you began teaching in the first place, I hope this book helps you to reignite it. Re-fall in love with this selfless way of life.

People are so quick to point out each other's differences or compare themselves to others. What unites us is simply being human. Experiencing a myriad of emotions in life. The reasons for each emotion might vary, but the emotion itself is one in the same. We have all felt excitement, joy, sadness, fear, emotional pain, and physical pain. You are not alone. What this world seems to lack is empathy, compassion, acceptance, and understanding.

Imagine what your classroom would be like if children grew up in a world where kindness took center stage. Allowing us to understand one another. In a world where differences always seem to be pointed out and judged, the secret is that we all have the capacity to love and create peace in our own life and in our world by living with compassion and empathy. By being the change we want to see in this damaged world.

I have always been fascinated by humankind and learning about what makes each person so unique. Our experiences in life, both good and bad, shape us into the people we are today. We are exposed to a negative world at such a young age. Violence and fear become all too familiar. The media tells us we have to act a certain way to be accepted, look a certain way to be attractive, and think a certain way to be considered right.

It is up to us to look beyond that and set an example of acceptance and kindness for others. Everyone is facing a battle you don't know about. Everyone is struggling to *look beyond the clouds* in their life. If you make the effort to understand a person's background and life story better, it is much easier to love and accept who they are. You will be more understanding of why that person acts a certain way, not making it acceptable but having the awareness of why, which then allows you to empathize with them.

Human beings are meant to help one another and spread kindness. We just seemed to get lost somewhere along the way. Live each day with the conscious decision to *look beyond the clouds* and live in the sunshine and help others do the same. That encouragement can make the greatest impact in the life of a fellow superstar, aka teacher.

"How does this apply to teaching and my classroom?" you may ask. It has *everything* to do with it. This change starts with us. With what our children learn in our classroom each day. Keep shining, the world needs your light.

## Self-Reflect

- Can you relate to Barbara's experiences? If so, how?
- Who is your teacher friend that you know you can turn to when your view is clouded and you need help reaching the sunshine beyond?
- Take note of the interactions you have with colleagues today. Do you provide them with the lift and light they yearn for?

# Take Action

- Be the lift and light your colleagues need and inspire them to continue the chain reaction. See how quickly that positivity can spread in your school.

- Choose to live in the sunshine and surround yourself with positivity, so you can live the fulfilled life you've always dreamed of—at work, at home, everywhere.

- Remember to put your own needs first, so you, in turn, can make an even greater impact on those around you.

- Continue to dig deep, face your fears head-on, self-reflect, and take action, all the while making time to nurture and care for yourself.

- Apply the concepts from this book to your teaching experiences as well as your personal life starting today. Enlist a friend or group of colleagues to join this movement with you. We can't do this alone.

# Afterword

Though our time together has come to an end (for now), it is my sincere hope that this book has inspired you to navigate the challenging world of teaching with positivity and gratitude. To address the growing issue of teacher burnout in your own life by adjusting your mindset. And to *look beyond the clouds* and choose to live in the sunshine. Not just today, but every day.

I hope it has helped you recognize the importance of acknowledging your own needs by mastering self-love and routinely engaging in self-care practices. Remember why you started teaching in the first place. Focus on the good in each day rather than getting caught up in the stress-filled atmosphere. Find joy in your work again and be recognized for the super human you are. Feel important, appreciated, cared for, supported, and understood.

This is only the beginning of your journey. Continue to dig deep and develop these positive, healthy habits in your daily life. Start the chain reaction that can come from changed reactions to situations at work. Face the upward climb of challenges head-on and strive to overcome them to reach your breathtaking view.

Think and speak positively. Spread that energy so you can inspire others to do the same. *Look beyond the clouds* that hinder your happiness. Explore the power of gratitude for each experience you are gifted and view each one as an opportunity to learn and grow. Push yourself to step out of your comfort zone and be open to change.

Light your world by giving other people the gift of your presence. Fall in love with the person in the mirror looking back at you who has been through so much but is still standing tall. Most importantly, remember to be patient with yourself. All of these habits take time to develop and become permanent. With perseverance and the right mindset, you can accomplish anything.

Now is the time to bring awareness to the issues teachers face that take over the morale of our schools. You deserve better. And so do your students. Let it begin with spreading the message of this positive movement. We can't do this alone.

To continue our time together, I would love to hear from you! Email me at michelle@lookbeyondtheclouds.com with the subject line, "Choosing to look beyond the clouds" or "Come speak in my district!"

Share your own stories and connections to the topics we've explored. Share the parts of the book that speak to you most and why. If you would like me to speak to the teachers in your district, let me know! I would love to meet and speak with as many fabulous teachers as I possibly can. Or simply email me to say hello and introduce yourself.

I look forward to spreading this positive movement with each of you.

Remember to visit my website for more support and opportunities:

www.lookbeyondtheclouds.com

# A Special Invitation

## Look Beyond the Clouds Community

Teachers who read *Look Beyond the Clouds* make up a remarkable group of like-minded individuals, who truly want to transform their daily habits, overcome the feelings of teacher burnout, and find joy in teaching again. Teachers often feel alone in their struggle to live in the sunshine. I challenge you to start the dialogue in your school, seek support from one other, and emerge from the isolation you feel in your mind.

As the creator of this positive movement, I want to invite you to join our online community and receive the support you deserve as you navigate through the challenging (yet beautiful and rewarding!) world of teaching.

In this community, you will:
- connect with other teachers,
- discuss the book,
- share the concepts and practices that helped you the most,
- post your own stories and experiences,
- be inspired and set your own goals,
- get encouragement, and
- find an accountability buddy.

Remember, you've got the powwwah to make positive changes in your life. Start your journey today! Join our *Look Beyond the Clouds Community* on Facebook. We look forward to welcoming you!

# Book Michelle to Speak!

## Book Michelle to speak at your next event!

Do the teachers in your school need help transforming their daily habits to overcome teacher burnout? Do they wish to clear their clouded view and feel joy in teaching again? Do they want to gain the much-needed recognition, appreciation, support, and understanding for the miracle work they do on a daily basis?

Email Michelle today at speaking@lookbeyondtheclouds.com!

Watch how quickly her inspiring stories and motivational words can spark a positive movement in *your* district.

- Professional Development Workshops
- College Education Departments
- Conferences
- Conventions
- And More!

For more info—visit www.lookbeyondtheclouds.com

# I'd Love to Hear from YOU!

## Thank you for reading my book!

I am grateful for your feedback and love hearing what you have to say. I need your input to make the next version of this book and my future books even better.

Please leave me a helpful review on Amazon letting me know what you thought of the book.

I really appreciate your most valuable resource—your time! Thank you for taking the time to read this book and invest in yourself to better your own life and the lives of everyone around you.

—Michelle Gano

# Michelle's Recs:
# Books, Music, and Beyond

Here's a list of all the media—books, music, movies, etc.—that I've mentioned in this book. I've organized the list based on the chapter where the particular media mention appears.

Introduction
- *Rent*: if you can't see this musical live, then watch a filmed version of it.

Chapter 2
- K-Love radio station

Chapter 3
- "The Climb" by Miley Cyrus

Chapter 4
- "The Power!" by Snap
- *Beauty and the Beast*

Chapter 5
- "Imagine" by John Lennon
- *Bubble Gum Brain* by Julia Cook

Chapter 6
- "A Whole New World" from Disney's *Aladdin*
- *Kisses From Katie* by Katie Davis

Chapter 7
- "All You Need Is Love" by the Beatles
- *The Five Love Languages: How to Express Heartfelt Commitment to Your Mate* by Gary Chapman
- *The Five Love Languages of Children* by Gary Chapman and Ross Campbell

Chapter 8
- "Go Light Your World" by Kathy Troccoli
- *Mean Girls*

Chapter 9
- "Livin' on a Prayer" by Bon Jovi

Chapter 11
- "Rise Up" by Andrea Day

# Acknowledgments

N ow is my time to shine the spotlight on the people behind the scenes who have helped shape the person I am today and helped make this book a dream come true. I am forever grateful for their endless support. (At least read the last one ... it's for you!)

I would like to start by thanking my incredible husband, Brandon—not only have you supported me in all of my dreams and adventures, you have filled my life with more love and happiness than I could have ever imagined. This book would not have been possible if it weren't for you. You encouraged me to chase this dream and stood by me every step of the way. You held me as I relived the strong emotions from past experiences reminding me that each story would help someone who needed it. Thank you for your endless support and encouragement. We have proven time and time again that together, we can accomplish anything. We are the strongest team I know. You will always be my greatest adventure.

To my baby boy, Brayden—I know you can't read this yet, but you played a very important part in writing this book. You were my motivation to keep going and accomplish this dream in time for your arrival. You were with me every step of the way giving many kicks to remind me why I was working so hard. Thank you for making my dreams of being a mommy come true. You are loved more than you will ever know, my sweet baby.

To my family—Mom, Dad, Billy, Erica, Jillian, Louie, my grandparents, aunts, uncles, and cousins—thank you for the immeasurable amount of love that you have always shown me. I am forever grateful for the memories we share. For those of you who share the same passion for teaching and have dedicated your lives to helping children, thank you for sharing your stories with me over the years. I am the person and teacher I am today because of each of you.

To my in-laws—Jim, Carol, and Colin—words can't even describe how lucky I feel to be part of your family. You accept me for the weird human I am and love me endlessly. Thank you for your unwavering support and encouragement.

To Brittany and Damien—whenever we're together our bond grows deeper. We've been open about our own clouds, but continuously encourage one another to reach for our dreams. You make my life brighter by being in it.

To my teacher friends—Diana, Kim, Angel, Katherine, and Melanie—I am so grateful for your friendship, which has turned us into a school family. You have been there for me during some of the most difficult experiences and helped me *look beyond the clouds.* Thank you for your love, support, and ceaseless laughter. It has brought such joy to my life!

To my teachers—Ms. Russo, Ms. Ahrens, Mrs. Bocchino, Dr. Pesavento, Dr. Medico-Letwinsky, and Ms. Skrutski—thank you for being such a positive influence in my life. You were so much more than teachers to me. You exemplified the teacher I dreamed of becoming. I honor you by showing my students the same love and concern you showed me.

To my students—you are my inspiration for all that I do. You motivate me to be the very best "school mommy" I can be for you. I will always be so proud of you and love you dearly.

To Self-Publishing School—Chandler Bolt, Lise Cartwright, and all SPS community members—thank you for helping me make this dream a reality. With your guidance and support, I became a published author in a short amount of time. I owe my success to you.

To Nancy Pile, Christos Angelidakis, and Debbie Lum—it has been such a pleasure having you part of my team as an editor, cover designer, and formatter. You have gone above and beyond to help make this book the best it can be. I look forward to working with you again on my future book writing adventures.

To my readers, you fabulous human beings—thank you for allowing me to be a part of your life and helping me spread this positive message to as many amazing teachers as possible. I hope it brings you the hope and joy you have been searching for in your career and personal life. May you feel recognized and appreciated for the miracle work you do every single day in your classroom. I look forward to welcoming you to the *Look Beyond the Clouds Community* on Facebook to interact with other like-minded teachers and immerse yourself in our much-needed positive support system.

# About the Author

Michelle Gano has dedicated her life to helping people see the good in the world. Through her example, she inspires others to navigate and overcome challenges with positivity, gratitude, and a strong foundation of self-love.

Michelle enjoys the simple moments in life like spending time with her husband, son, and puppy. As a teacher, she has touched the lives of countless students and families over the years. She teaches beyond academics and makes sure her students feel loved and cared for. With her guidance, they learn the importance of being kind, setting goals, working toward their dreams, persevering regardless of obstacles, and most importantly, loving themselves and others unconditionally.

Today, Michelle is an author and motivational speaker for teachers and children. She is determined to bring awareness to the issues teachers face in their often-thankless careers. Her positive movement, *Look Beyond the Clouds*, helps teachers find joy in their work again and gain recognition for the super humans they are. Her goal is to help as many teachers as possible feel important, appreciated, cared for, supported, and understood.

This is only the beginning for Michelle. She plans to write more inspirational and motivational books to help more people *look beyond the clouds*. She plans to write children's books to reinforce lessons that will help lead them to positive, fulfilling lives.

~

To learn more about Michelle's *Look Beyond the Clouds Movement*, to book Michelle as a speaker at your school, or simply to share a story with her or ask a question, please visit:

www.lookbeyondtheclouds.com or
email her at michelle@lookbeyondtheclouds.com.

If you are looking to interact with other like-minded teachers and immerse yourself in a positive support system, Michelle invites you to join the *Look Beyond the Clouds Community* on Facebook.

Made in the USA
Middletown, DE
23 May 2022

66106188R00120